Paul Taylor and Vicki Taylor

The WILDERNESS Way

Twelve Foundational Stones for Building Unshakable Faith in a Chaotic World

Second Edition

Paul Taylor and Vicki Taylor

The WILDERNESS Way

Twelve Foundational Stones for Building Unshakable Faith in a Chaotic World

Second Edition

With

ACKNOWLEDGMENTS

All praise and glory to the real Author of *The Wilderness Way*, the Lord Jesus Christ and His blessed Holy Spirit, who accomplishes His purpose through common men and women.

We would also like to acknowledge and thank Kimberly Shumate of ReVision Editing Agency, for working with us so diligently to refine the book's material.

We'd also like to thank Jean Liu Christen of 8C Entertainment, for guiding this project through each step of the publishing process.

We're forever grateful.

THE WILDERNESS WAY
Copyright ©2025 by Pastor Paul Taylor and Vicki Taylor
Published by Wilderness Way

www.thewildernessway.com

Distributed by Redemption Press
www.redemptionpress.com

All rights reserved. No part of this publication may be reproduced, stored in a retrieval system, or transmitted in any form or by any means—electronic, mechanical, digital, photocopy, recording, or any other—except for brief quotations in printed reviews, without the prior permission of the publisher.

All Scripture quotations are taken from the New King James Version.
Copyright © 1982 by Thomas Nelson, Inc. Used by permission. All rights reserved.

ABOUT THE COVER

The man coming out of the wilderness, walking toward the living waters is Johnny Buscema. He is as a son to us and a benefactor to the Wilderness Way. It has been our joy and privilege to come alongside him as he built his foundation in Christ through the word of God. We are beyond grateful for his loving support of our ministry.

Behold, I will do a new thing,
Now it shall spring forth;
Shall you not know it?
I will even make a road in the wilderness
And rivers in the desert.

ISAIAH 43:19

Special thanks to Fulvia Santoni for the cover photography and images throughout the book and to Michael Macaluso for contributing His expertise to the book cover.

Contents

Acknowledgments 2

About the cover 3

A Note for Leaders 8

Introduction: Finding My Way 9

The Cornerstone 15

Stone #1: Truth 21

Stone #2: Obedience 43

Stone #3: Glory 65

Stone #4: Love 85

Stone #5: Wisdom 107

Stone #6: Discernment 123

Stone #7: Humility 137

Stone #8: Self-Control 153

Stone #9: Perseverance 167

Stone #10: Forgiveness 179

Stone #11: Repentance 197

Stone #12: Security 213

Salvation 229

A NOTE FOR LEADERS

Welcome to *The Wilderness Way*! It's our deepest wish and prayer that you and your group will be encouraged, educated, and inspired to grow in your faith and the knowledge of God through the twelve stones presented in this biblical study.

The Wilderness Way is ideally taught with a group introductory session, followed by twelve additional sessions that examine one stone per week. You might want to plan a food fellowship for the initial session—if the size of the group allows—as it is our intention for everyone to feel at ease and excited about the study. Once you've distributed the workbooks and have familiarized folks with the weekly format, everyone should be on the same page!

In the months to come, members will enjoy private weekly study in preparation for the coming discussion. If it's a large group, you may decide to appoint several leaders and break into smaller cell groups for a more personal discussion time. We've found that one-hour sessions work well, with half of the time dedicated to discussion (of the previous week's stone) followed by the leader's teaching of the current week's stone. Of course, you're free to adjust this structure to fit the needs of your church or study group.

As friendships are formed and strengthened through the small group time, an intimate, interactive, and relaxed sharing of unity and love will prevail. We pray that God uses *The Wilderness Way* to foster a sense of reenergized community that feeds the faith of your congregation and those drawn into its light.

Scripture references for *The Wilderness Way* are from the New King James Version (NKJV) of the Bible. For clarity, we encourage you to follow along with the same version.

Additional resources available:

- *The Wilderness Way for 55+* is designed to encourage seniors to continue striving toward their goal in Jesus Christ (based on the twelve stones), thus leaving a legacy of faith through journaling for future generations to read.

- *The Wilderness Way for Children* is a complete guide to teaching kids the same stones at their own level.

- *The Wilderness Way — Small Group Study*, Twelve Foundational Stones for Building Unshakable Faith in a Chaotic World invites readers to a 25-week journey through the biblical definitions and impact of words essential to the Christian faith.

INTRODUCTION

Finding My Way

For it is not a futile thing for you, because it is your life, and by this word you shall prolong your days in the land which you cross over the Jordan to possess.

DEUTERONOMY 32:47

One of my greatest joys in being a pastor is leading others to Christ. Some come to Him with a river of tears, showing intense emotion. Others pray with a quiet commitment in their voice. Some can only find the courage to repeat the prayer of repentance. But no matter the words or way, if one is sincere in their faith, the miracle of salvation and filling of the Holy Spirit occurs, and the journey begins.

From children to adults, leading souls to Christ is one of the greatest privileges of ministry. So likewise, there is nothing sadder for a pastor than to see the joy of salvation fade due partly to a failure to build a foundation on Christ and His Word.

So, what happens? Why do new believers become disillusioned, discouraged, drift away, or stall? They are missing the strong foundation that transforms them from baby Christians to powerful, effective men and women of God.

For new Christians to survive and thrive, they must begin building a relationship with Christ based upon His Word. Mere Christian activity cannot replace the precious journey of building a relationship with Christ, stone by stone. While the church does all it can to help new believers on their way, it is the responsibility of each individual to build a personal relationship with their champion, their friend, Jesus.

Although I was initially unaware, *The Wilderness Way* began when a young man asked me to mentor him, and I agreed. As I prepared each week, God started laying foundational words, or "stones," on my heart—one week at a time, stone after stone. Soon, our 5 a.m. weekly study grew from one to six men, and *The Wilderness Way* emerged. I have since spent countless hours studying, teaching, and preaching the value of these powerful words to my own congregation as well as many other churches.

I drew the title from the Israelites' exodus from Egypt. What God intended to be a two-year journey for His people became a lifelong struggle of wandering through the wilderness, never experiencing the abundance God so desired to pour out on them. When God took His children out of Egypt by a great miracle, He led them straight into the wilderness, where they would witness God's tenderness, miracles, and provision for them. They needed time with God, free from distractions, to know their Creator intimately, and so do we. However, as Christians, let us be careful not to wander into a faith wasteland as the Israelites did.

The tragedy for the Israelites, and even many Christians today, seems to be that they are wandering. They may fail to embrace time in the wilderness with God—a special measured season of preparation for service. Or they spend a lifetime there, and never fully experience God or the upward journey He desires for them.

It would be wise of us to learn from those who have come before us, setting the example:

- **Paul**—Before his startling conversion, he was known as Saul, highly educated and ruthless when it came to the treatment of new believers of Jesus. Still, he spent three years in the desert learning, shedding his old self, building a foundation in Christ. When his time there was complete, he returned as the "apostle Paul" to begin a ministry that would last the rest of his life and touch every future Christian on earth.

- **Moses**—A vulnerable child born into poverty and elevated to royalty, he became a murderer. Forced to run, Moses left everything and fled into the wilderness to hide. Forty years would pass before his burning bush experience. Enough time to think, pray, and learn lessons that his privileged life in Egypt couldn't teach him. Moses would emerge from his wilderness experience to lead a nation from impoverished captivity and become a foreshadow of Christ.

- **Elijah**—The great prophet of old, who could pray down rain and fire from heaven, found himself in the wilderness, where he learned to love, trust, and rely on God more fully. Elijah reappeared from the wilderness empowered by God to raise a child from the dead, and was given the distinction of being called "a man of God."

Let us never forget that God has more for us than we can imagine. And sometimes, the wilderness of life is the only place where we will find our greater calling and purpose.

Speaking from my own experience, when I finally surrendered my life to Jesus as an adult, I was not fond of reading. Yet, I became ravenous for God's Word—to immerse myself, learning all I possibly could about Him. To sit in His presence. To listen to His wisdom. To feel His embrace. To know I was His. Few things can fill a person with gratitude as the undeniable understanding of just how cherished they are. To belong to God. To be exposed to the true origin of love and know that they were made from it. It is a gift like no other.

While I attended and enjoyed BSF (Bible Study Fellowship) Bible study, it wasn't enough to satisfy my hunger for God. Between work and family, the only time to dive deep into His Word was from eleven at night and on, eventually stumbling into bed exhausted. These late-night studies continued for the next ten years. But that midnight wilderness with the Lord prepared me to become an ordained minister and servant of Jesus.

A desert well worth the energy, solitude, and commitment.

Make no mistake, dear friend: God has a special time in the wilderness just for you. A preordained period of time when He will build a powerful, everlasting, life-changing foundation in Him, if you will heed the invitation. A time that will give your life purpose and meaning beyond your own limited dreams and ambitions, all for His glory.

I believe the truths found in the twelve stones we'll be focusing on, once embedded firmly into your faith, will become fertile soil, making the Word of God rich with meaning. Beyond this, it's my hope that this powerful prose will find a home deep within you, bringing a new perspective to common verbs that would otherwise be dulled by the world and its thin interpretations.

God challenges us to not only be "hearers" of the Word, but also "doers" of the Word (James 1:22). Paraphrased, don't let your salvation sit idle like a trophy on a shelf, but allow God to use it in magnificent ways, a spectacle of His will and His work. Jesus is "The Word"—the Sword of the Spirit—and as active and insatiable as you concede Him to be.

The foundational stones of spiritual growth captured in the pages of this book can and will bring a needed maturity and steadfastness to your temple—your body, mind, and soul—if you will take the time to receive, polish, and build upon them.

At the end of each chapter, you'll find a space to record what the Spirit has taught you and how He has challenged and encouraged you to adjust your life. Be prayerful in your studies, and reflect those holy in your comments.

Wherever you see "Got it!", write down your thoughts. These "Got it!" revelations will offer clarity and encouragement to others in your study group and will be vital to the evolution of your own personal foundation.

> *Therefore, thus says the Lord God: "Behold, I lay in Zion*
> *a stone for a foundation, a tried stone, a precious cornerstone,*
> *a sure foundation; whoever believes will not act hastily."*
>
> **ISAIAH 28:16**

It's fascinating to think there can be a difference of 1,200 miles between a compass' magnetic north and true north, the North Star. As surely as that sparkling point of light shines, giving us solid direction, Jesus is also our North Star, guiding us by His Holy Spirit. However, just like the draw of a magnet, Satan's pull of deception can lead us away from true north, many times without us even being aware. The Bible and the Holy Spirit are our only reliable guides and moral compasses.

Wherever you see this symbol ( ), please take note of an important principle. These are essential truths that will guide you true north throughout this study.

Jesus is our true north!

Above all this, before we begin studying these words of life, I ask that you have the Cornerstone set firmly in place—that is, Jesus Christ—for the weight of all other stones rests upon it. The Cornerstone is supreme; His design is unequaled. The strength of your spiritual house will always rely on the foundation you lay.

If there is a doubt in your mind as to the authenticity of your cornerstone, I trust you will skip ahead to the final chapter titled "Salvation" before proceeding to the spiritual stones.

May God bless the study of His word.

The Cornerstone

Now, therefore, you are no longer strangers and foreigners, but fellow citizens with the saints and members of the household of God, having been built on the foundation of the apostles and prophets, Jesus Christ Himself being the chief cornerstone, in whom the whole building, being fitted together, grows into a holy temple in the Lord.

EPHESIANS 2:19-21

When Vicki and I began writing *The Wilderness Way*, it was important to us to impress upon leaders and readers that the twelve stones studied in this book are solely based on the chief Cornerstone, Jesus. These byproducts, when fixed within the foundation of our faith, serve to strengthen our relationship with God, with His Son, and with the Holy Spirit, enriching our Christian walk as we continue to build upon the Cornerstone that is Christ.

But what are the twelve foundational stones, and how do they directly affect us?

As God's **truth** takes its rightful position in our minds, hearts, and lives, **obedience** to Him is the natural result. Our reborn state prevents us from continuing in our old path of self-destructive patterns. This can only **glorify** God as the Creator of all truth. He accomplishes this by agape love, which is as much a part of our human makeup as He is our spiritual genetic Father.

While His **love** seeps into our very bones, **wisdom** sprouts up as **discernment** reveals it. Perhaps the stone that compels us to surrender self in no uncertain terms is that of **humility**. It requires us to lay down the last of our power to accept whatever comes—all things being funneled through Jesus. In every circumstance, we are to bow to the one who teaches the futility of mortal control. This allows **self-control** to mindfully, deliberately practice good, God-honoring Christian behavior.

It is this change that enables us to act and react in a more Godly way, and in doing so, the enemy will attempt to disrupt our faith's forward progress. Though times of trial may appear cruel, **perseverance** will have its perfect work—a stone that persistently holds our faith in place. Within this divine patience, we hone the gift of **forgiveness** as we realize just how much we have been forgiven by God. This forgiveness remains in effect as long as we are breathing.

Repentance is yet another permanent stone that must stay in place all of our days, as we continually tell God we are sorry for our offenses (as we are convicted), and to forgive our faults as we recognize and forgive the faults of others. Since we cannot live perfectly, we should *forgive, repent… repeat.*

Lastly, the stone of **security** is one that closely reflects the Cornerstone, that is Jesus. He is our high tower, our fortress, our shelter in the storm. This realization helps us define who we are in Him, and how much authority we have over conditions and the giants who have so easily ensnared us in the past. Nothing under heaven can stop the plans God has for us. In this, we are secure.

> *I have come that [you] may have life,*
> *and that [you] may have it more abundantly.*
> **JOHN 10:10**

Perhaps by reading this book, you will rediscover your confidence in salvation, and come to realize the importance of fortifying a firm foundation in Christ. May you gain a greater appreciation for the truth of His Word, and a reenergized conviction to pursue His plans for you.

Let's examine what the evidence of a strong foundation in Christ looks like:

1. You know God personally and experientially. (Ephesians 3:17-19)
2. You serve the Lord through the gifts He has entrusted to you. (1 Peter 4:10)
3. You are willing to help others. (Galatians 6:2; Hebrews 13:16)
4. You are committed to the Lord's work through tithes, believing your leap of faith will be blessed. (Mark 12:43-44)

There are no shortcuts to a Christ-centered life, but nothing is more worthy of the pursuit. Our family life, church life, and the image of God others see in us are all intimately connected. With salvation should come an awareness that we are the hands and feet of Jesus.

The depth you choose to delve into the character of Jesus will ultimately become the strength or weakness of your foundation. So let's look at the evidence of a weak foundation:

1. Self-desire wins over obedience to God, over and over
2. A life defeated by circumstance
3. Little to no learning or growing in Christ

Always remember that it's never too late to get honest with God or serious about your foundation. Like anything being built that reaches for the sky, the higher the structure, the deeper the base. Its groundwork establishes its strength, beauty, and longevity. Such is the Word of God.

> *For it is not a futile thing for you, because it is your life, and by this word you shall prolong your days in the land which you cross over the Jordan to possess."*
>
> **DEUTERONOMY 32:47**

This verse hangs in our church's entryway. I have jokingly remarked that we should have a sign that reads "ENTER AT YOUR OWN RISK" instead. But the truth is, it is no joke—there is no flirting with Jesus or taking His words lightly. However, if we make His Word our words; if we adopt His work as our work, then we are true disciples and will live long, passion-filled lives in the ministry of His making.

Embrace the twelve stones we will cover in this book and wrestle them into their rightful place in your life. Set them with the mortar of prayer. Once embedded as your own moral compass, they will guide and protect you. May they become part of who you are and everything you do.

> *Let your light so shine before men, that they may see your good works and glorify your Father in heaven.*
>
> **MATTHEW 5:16**

A bible that is falling apart often belongs to a person who isn't. Its truth will change your life from the inside out.

Got It!

Take a moment to reflect on the twelve stones I've mentioned. Which one(s) do you struggle with the most? Which of them are most meaningful to you?

STONE #1

Truth

In the Beginning was the Word, and the Word was with God, and the Word was God.

JOHN 1:1

What comes to mind when you think about the word "truth"? Most likely, you find it to be a rational conclusion after thoughtfully looking at all the evidence, along with a dash of discernment. However, the Bible tells us that truth has a single name, and that name is Jesus: "I am…the truth." (John 14:6).

In declaring himself the great "I Am," the ultimate statement of self-sufficiency and self-existence, Jesus is stating that He is not bound by anyone or any circumstance. He is and always will be the eternally constant God, unchangeable and completely sufficient in Himself.

When "I AM" proclaims himself the way, the truth, and the life, asserting that no one comes to the Father except through Him, it is an absolute nonnegotiable fact that no force in existence can alter. Human thoughts and feelings are irrelevant. Every soul that has ever lived will carve out their eternal destiny through this one, profound statement.

The following story attests to the power of this truth.

Danie Jay, a YouTube strategist and coach, grew up in a Christian home, but strayed into New Age practices after college. Convinced that there were many paths to God, she went on a journey of exploration. She eventually found herself lying on a bed as a shaman performed a ceremony over her—one that would confirm the power to heal others. Interesting enough, what jolted her back to God's truth was a simple act—when the shaman closed the blinds, which blocked out the light.

> *Then Jesus spoke to them again, saying, "I am the light
> of the world. He who follows Me shall not walk in darkness,
> but have the light of life."*
> **JOHN 8:12**

According to Danie's testimony, that was the moment the blinders ("scales") were removed from her spiritual eyes, and she could see the darkness for what it was—evil. Too frightened to stop the ceremony, she lay there praying until the ritual ended. Afterward, the shaman appeared shaken. Still, she assured her that she was uniquely special with the ability to heal people in every way.

It was then that she finally understood there was a fight for her soul, the soul that had accepted Jesus as a child. She confessed that she had made herself her own god. Later, alone in her room, she returned to her roots by praying, "I choose Jesus," thus bringing her journey full circle.

I'd like you to read John 14:17-18 and answer the questions below:

What keeps the world from receiving the Spirit of truth?

Who does the Spirit of truth dwell in?

What does God promise He will never do?

The Spirit of truth had not left Danie Jay (His child) an orphan, even in all the years she spent in the wilderness. He had been with her every step of her journey, which led her back to Him with new conviction. Whatever you believe about God's truth, it cannot equal the actual power of it. It fiercely protects God's own, and is filled with love and compassion. I encourage you to listen to her complete testimony on YouTube, titled "New Age to Jesus Testimony."

> *The Christian does not think God will love us because we are good,*
> *but that God will make us good because He loves us.*
>
> **C.S. LEWIS**

When Jesus stood before Pilate in what would be the final hours of His life, Truth was put to the test. The last three years had been filled with nonstop ministry and miracles, and many in the region came to believe in Him as their long-awaited Savior—the true Son of God. Now, standing in the presence of Rome's governor of Judaea as well as Israel's religious leaders, Jesus would be taken to task for His contemptible words and conduct. His very being. The answer He gave to them, recorded in the Book of John, 18:37, was a simple one:

> "I have come into the world, that I should bear witness to the truth. Everyone who is of the truth hears My voice."

In Pilate's frustration, he retorted, "What is truth?"

These same words have echoed repeatedly throughout the ages ever since. I don't believe there has ever been a time in history when God's truth has been considered more irrelevant than it is today. In a society where a fetus isn't a baby, and children are free to choose their own gender, the word "truth" and its meaning is continually up for debate. The fact is, no truth is absolute in the minds of those who lack spiritual understanding and dismiss their conscious need for God.

It all starts with denying just one truth—that Jesus Christ is King. If Jesus is not King, then His Word is irrelevant, and truth is subject to whatever facts one chooses. Just as it was written in Judges 21:25, "In those days there was no king in Israel; everyone did what was right in his own eyes," it seems things haven't changed at all.

Pilate's response was similar to many today who claim to have the undeniable truth, yet when those truths contradict each other, they throw up their hands in disgust and question, "What is truth?" Well, let's think about it for a minute.

We know that God's truth never changes—it is fixed and perfect. That means it never lies due to its flawless nature. Nothing to add. Nothing to take away. It is complete just as it is. However, progressive theology suggests that God (or what it sees as God or the Creator of the Universe) is in a state of flux. That it is constantly maturing, morphing, growing as a "work in progress." Yet the Bible says there is no variation or "shadow of turning" with God (James 1:17; John 8:32).

God is not who we think He is.
He's who He says He is.

Take a moment to ponder the following questions. See if you can find in Scripture, what truth is and what it is not. Come to terms with the unshakable elements of God's truth, and commit to memory a verse or verses that boil down the essence of His divine reliability.

1. How important is it that we believe God's Word to be an absolute, unchanging truth? (Genesis 2:17; 3:1-10)

2. The greatest obstacle to overcome for an unbeliever is accepting Jesus and God's Word as total truth. What are the human aspects that keep a person from believing in Christ and all that He represents? (John 18:38; Psalm 10:4)

3. Truth must be the starting point for every believer. What are some of the reasons why folks are unable to trust God's truth? What is it that frightens, worries, or concerns them? (John 1:5-9; 1 John 3:18)

_____

_____

_____

4. Truth determines a person's moral compass, which directly determines their character. If Jesus' character was an extension of His truth—His moral compass—how can we reflect that same truth as followers of Christ? (John 8:28-29)

_____

_____

_____

To follow Christ, one must believe that every word of the Bible is true. In this way, we give the enemy zero room to plant seeds of doubt or to distort God's perfect narrative. We find the Holy Spirit abiding in every phrase and in every promise, which leaves no vacuum to fill or loose threads to tie up.

To follow Christ, one must believe that every word of the Bible is true.

The entirety of Your word is truth, and every one of Your righteous judgments endures forever.

PSALM 119:160

How many people, do you suppose, ever take the time to thoughtfully consider the origin and history of the Bible? Some of us say, "God said it, so that settles it!" But other folks like the apostle Thomas argue, "Unless I see in His hands the print of the nails… and put my hand into

His side, I will not believe" (John 20:25). Thus, it would be more likely for those unbelievers to expect they'll be struck by lightning than accept the One who makes the lightning flash and the thunder rumble.

After his wife's conversion to Christianity, a journalist and atheist named Lee Strobel set out to prove the Bible was a lie. We can only imagine the passionate conversations the couple must have had to encourage such a pursuit on his part. But as he explored the evidence, Strobel became a believer in 1981, and there ended the dispute.

This certainly wasn't the first pursuit of the truth by someone who felt their personal beliefs would outweigh the contrasting opinion; though I suspect that most journeys conclude with the same ending when their case is met with overwhelming biblical evidence. The Book's history, archaeology, contents (including prophesy and eyewitness accounts) all attest to the truth of God's Word. To travel into the evidence of the Bible is to wade into deep waters of authenticity, which can't help but open unbelieving eyes and soften hardened hearts.

It's much easier for the Spirit to enter through the open door of an accepting house than to fight a padlock of resistance in a prison of self-serving denial. But for argument's sake, let's discuss some of the sticking points and the truth behind what can cause confusion or even animosity regarding the Bible.

THE BIBLE'S HISTORY

When we examine the Bible's sixty-six books, we know that it was written over the span of approximately 1,500 years by 40 writers. These human transcribers of God's Word range from Moses to Solomon; Isaiah to Jeremiah; Ezekiel to Daniel; and that's just some of the Old Testament books. The New Testament includes such spiritual powerhouses as Matthew, Mark, Luke, John, Peter, and Jude (brother of Jesus and James), not to be outdone by the Apostle Paul who wrote the vast majority of letters to the early church. The Bible tells a consistent story: God, who created all mankind, desires to have a personal relationship with us, asking us to love and trust Him. It's a message that doesn't get much simpler than that. I said simple, not easy.

In 2012, the Business Insider stated that with 3.9 billion copies sold in the last 50 years, the Bible was and is the most-read book globally[1]. That's an extraordinary number considering five decades

---

1. www.businessinsider.com/the-top-10-most-read-books-in-the-world-infographic-2012-12

ago in 1960, the world's population hit 3 billion, which caused a cultural frenzy making the cover story of *Time Magazine* titled, "That Population Explosion." Seems like the good old days now as we look over our shoulder from 2024 and our present 8+ billion souls that inhabit the planet.

The survival of the Bible through the ages would be tough to explain if it weren't the truth. A lie would have been unearthed, pounced on, and ripped apart before being scattered to the wind. Books are like dying creatures with only a tiny percentage of them surviving longer than twenty years, with most lasting just a couple of print runs and then forgotten. If you don't believe me, just for fun, check to see how many titles Amazon has in its archive. The amount of content written, printed, stored, and summarily dismissed is mind-blowing. But among the rotting ruins of all that literary treasure and garbage, only one book has stood the test of time and turmoil—the Bible.

Over the centuries, those who have sought to abolish the Bible and extinguish its flame have failed. Divine intervention has always won while the impenetrable truth that the Bible contains is indestructible and proves time and again that its Author cannot lie.

THE BIBLE'S ARCHAEOLOGY

In the spring of 2019, during our two-week visit to Israel, from early morning to late evening, the church group we were traveling with was shuffled from one archaeological biblical site to another until we were nearly overwhelmed by truth.

To stand in the Garden of Gethsemane, overlooking the Kedron Valley and the ancient Eastern Gate of Old Jerusalem, is mind-blowing. There we were, eyewitnesses to the remains of the Pool of Bethesda, reading about the healing of the disabled man. We walked the terrace of King David's palace depicted in 2 Samuel 11:2. As the Scripture entails, it overlooks the rooftops of Jerusalem, where he saw Bathsheba bathing. We visited the cave where Bedouin teenagers discovered the Dead Sea Scrolls, including the entire book of Isaiah. The feeling was surreal.

They say that if you stick a shovel in the ground of the Holy Land, you come up with archaeological treasure, but it is slow, tedious work in constant need of financing. Nevertheless, the evidence of biblical people, places, and things brings one to the conclusion that its Author cannot be denied.

THE BIBLE'S PROPHECY

What if I told you that writings, completed in 450 B.C., hundreds of years before Jesus's birth, contained over 300 prophecies that Jesus fulfilled through His life, death, and resurrection? Since history and archaeology prove they occurred, would anyone be able to effectively, legitimately dispute or discount them? What convincing evidence or argument could they pose to delegitimize the hard facts?

In *Science Speaks*, written by Peter Stoner, the mathematical odds of any single person fulfilling even 8 of the 300 prophecies at random was estimated to be 1 in 100,000,000,000,000,000. That's one quadrillion or a thousand million million to you and me. Therefore, science itself backs the undisputable odds that the Bible's Author does not predict blindly.

THE BIBLE'S EYEWITNESSES

Whether we're talking about the past or present, eyewitnesses hold significant weight in a court of law. Moreover, our world chronology and knowledge are all contained within historical records initially written or described by firsthand observers. Then why is it the world is so quick to refute eyewitnesses of biblical accounts?

It is also written in your law that the testimony
of two men is true.
JOHN 8:17

According to the historical record, Moses was there when the Red Sea parted and later wrote of his experience. In the New Testament, the witnesses to the crucifixion included the Apostle John who wrote about it in stunning detail. His cohort, Luke, who wrote the Book of Acts, gives a written account in the first chapter of the risen Jesus. This information is confirmed by further eyewitness accounts of those who saw Jesus alive after His earthly death—by more than 500 people on twelve separate occasions (1 Corinthians 15:3-8). This number of bystanders to affirm the facts leaves no choice but to reconcile that the Bible's truth is to be believed, and that its Author is divine.

And being fully convinced that what [God] had promised
He was also able to perform.
ROMANS 4:21

I was raised in a Christian home during the 60s and taken to church whenever the doors were open—they were open quite a lot back then! I learned about the Bible in Sunday school, was sent to camp every summer, and professed faith in Jesus Christ at age twelve. And yet, from the ages of 17 to 40, I chose to wander far from God into the wilderness. Even so, I cannot remember a time when I questioned God's biblical truth. But something was missing.

It's one thing to believe the Word of God is altogether true, but it is quite another to recognize and apply it as a building block in your life. I needed a profound truth, an active truth, the kind that rocks your world and leaves you trembling at the deity of Jesus. I needed the kind of truth that Peter experienced.

Read Matthew 16:13-19, and answer the questions below.

1. What two questions did Jesus ask His disciples?

2. What was their response?

3. Since Jesus is all-knowing, why do you believe He asked these questions?

4. How easily influenced are you by others' opinions of Christianity?

5. Are you ever tempted to take the less controversial view for fear of seeming too conservative or judgmental?

6. Why do you believe Jesus pressed the question further, and what was Peter's response?

7. Who does Jesus say revealed this profound truth to Peter?

Did the questions that Jesus posed to His disciples seem odd? After all, they had been with Jesus for some time and witnessed countless miracles. Knowing Him as we do today—with the benefit of the completed Bible as well as our personal relationship and indwelling of the Holy Spirit—we understand that Jesus never asked a question in vain. But what did the apostles think about His queries? Surely they were a test; a test none of them wanted to fail.

Upon their arrival in the region of Caesarea Philippi, Jesus asked His followers, "Who do the people say I am?" Their first response was safe, especially being Jewish. "Some say John the Baptist while others say Elijah, and others say Jeremiah or one of the prophets." No doubt, these close friends of Jesus believed in Him. But to declare that He was the Messiah meant laying down their veil of Jewish tradition to pick up the new cloak of Christianity, albeit a precursor to the finished work of Christ we embrace now.

But what of the second question: "Who do *you* say I am?"

Questions have a way of marking important moments. "Will you marry me?" is a good example. It sets in stone a date that will be remembered forever—either fondly or in infamy. The day Jesus asked His second, more direct question, Simon Peter's declaration changed everything including his life and the lives of those that surrounded him. He would later be put to death for that testimonial. Simon Peter confessed with his mouth: "You are the Messiah, the Son of the living God." Now he's committed; no turning back. And his assertion was so drastic that Jesus changed his name.

Like Abram to Abraham, and Sarai to Sarah, Jesus marked the event of this spiritual transformation, removing Simon (which means "hearer of the Word of God") leaving only the name Peter (which means "a rock"). It was Jesus's way of labeling him for future endeavors. A renewed identity that invoked the stability of a cornerstone on which a structure relies.

And it was there in the town of Caesarea Philippi where Jesus first commissioned His disciples to build His church—the collective body of Christ. Is it any wonder that He chose this location to erect His temple of flesh and blood? To this day, there is a cave tucked into the base of a cliff, where spring waters still flow. In the time of Jesus, the pagans living there believed the cave created a gateway to the underworld where fertility gods resided during the winter. They thought that their city was literally at the gates of hell, and would engage in perverse sexual acts each spring to entice the return of their god, Pan.

It was during our springtime trip to Israel in 2019 when Vicki and I toured the area. What a surreal feeling it was to stand beside that stream, gazing up at the cave marked "The Gates of Hell," reading "And the gates of Hades shall not prevail against it" written in bold red letters. Quite a statement when considering Jesus spoke these words over Peter to announce his new position on earth and in the spirit.

Teach me Your way, O Lord; I will walk in Your truth;
Unite my heart to fear Your name.
PSALM 86:11

Believing the gospel is one thing; having its truth captivate your soul until you are changed from the inside out is quite another. It's true, Vicki and I have been blessed a hundred times over thanks to God and all He has done for us and through us. But our faith didn't happen overnight. It is a slow burn; a flame that is lit, the lamp trimmed with constant prayer, study, and fellowship with true believers. God designed us for community with others and communion with Him, so that together we would find our whole selves amid unity and love.

Believing the gospel is one thing, having its truth captivate your soul is another.

From 1 John 2:3, what is the tangible evidence of a true believer?

According to 3 John 1:3-4, what was it that gave John the Evangelist "no greater joy"?

As we saturate our mind with God's truth, we will be challenged to leave behind our own worldly, misguided truth. As people God has divinely appointed to teach and lead others into His truth, we must learn to walk therein. Our journey requires all three—reading the Word, surrendering our own agendas, and purposefully operating in God's truth.

From Galatians 5:16, how do we avoid walking in the flesh?

What motivation does 1 John 2:6 give us for walking in the Spirit?

What is truth? It is that light that shines brightly in the certainty of God and all He has for us. His facts are our reality. He is worthy of our complete devotion, trust, and relinquishment of our lives because there is no one greater to believe in. He is perfect, omnipotent, omnipresent, and well able to keep all of His promises. He cannot lie, His history cannot be denied, and His prophecy is not blind. Everything He says will come to pass, "Not by might nor by power, but by My Spirit" (Zechariah 4:6), and God will accomplish all that He sets out to do.

Truth is the character of Jesus Christ, manifested to us through the Holy Spirit so that we can understand the importance of accepting His truth alone. Then, and only then, can we hope to walk through this life as disciples of Christ, separating His absolute truth from the world's hypotheticals.

The truth you believe in is the truth you will walk in.

In everyone's life, there will be a major decision that challenges us to stretch in a new and sometimes uncomfortable direction. That proverbial fork in the road where our well-laid plans are thrown to the wind, and God takes us on an unexpected journey of ministry, we feel completely ill-equipped to handle. When we would rather continue following our own itinerary and goals with everything neatly mapped out, God in His predictable unpredictability offers something different, something a little terrifying. But He's God and we're not. So, enough said.

The story of The Crossing, our church plant, is implausible when you view it from afar. Yet, here we are today, more than a decade later, going strong. How did we manage it when I never aspired to become a pastor? At the time God began to reveal His plan, I was working diligently to become an evangelist. That means leaving home—whether visiting areas domestically or traveling the globe to foreign lands. From the time I surrendered my life to Jesus, I wanted to tell the world about God's wondrous love for them and since I never dreamed I'd become a pastor, I set my heart on evangelism.

So when a friend told me about an empty church building in Nineveh, Indiana, I had two thoughts: *Where is Nineveh?* and *Not interested!* However, over the next couple of weeks, I kept hearing "go to Nineveh." You know that holy nudge when your spirit feels a quiet yet non-negotiable push that no inner debate or outer excuses can quell? And it's futile to resist when your fate is forged by God, so Vicki and I finally climbed into the car and were off to Nineveh.

When we pulled into the parking lot, it was not what we were expecting. I don't know *what* we were expecting, but not this. Maybe an older, less attractive, somewhat disheveled structure that had seen better days. What we did find was a lovely, almost new building that checked about every box.

"This would be a God thing," we said in unison, not believing it but absolutely believing it.

With nothing more than a phone call, we took possession without any money down or even providing as much as a social security number. Within a short time, we had a church. And I was petrified.

Having never pastored a church before, I wasn't even sure I could preach a sermon every Sunday. In addition to that, we had no "core" group of people to build upon and with limited finances to ready the church, it was a "God, you're going to have to do this" moment.

Signing up for a crash course in church planting through the Southern Baptist Convention, I found encouragement. It turned out that they were teaching many of the things God had already laid on my heart to pursue. Then God started sending people.

> *Establish the work of our hands for us;*
> *Yes, establish the work of our hands.*
>
> **PSALM 90:17**

With a few faithful friends who believed in our call, Vicki and I armed ourselves with eighty gallons of paint and got to work. To our surprise, the building that appeared to be in good condition on the outside was actually in disrepair and needed more TLC than expected. We watched as our finances quickly dwindled—such are the early days of any startup church. But these were simple opportunities for God to show us His tender willingness to provide.

We remain eternally grateful for every individual who answered God's call, allowing Him to work through them in building The Crossing. With fresh paint on the walls and contemporary chairs replacing the pink pews, opening Sunday arrived.

Unorthodox. Peculiar. Eccentric. Any of those words could describe our introduction of The Crossing to the town of Nineveh. With suitcases of every size and shape piled near the door, we would challenge our new congregants to "leave their baggage" at the door to step into the joyous freedom Christ offers. Labeled "legalism," "fear," "addiction," "apathy," and so on, the bags represented more than human struggles. They painted a grim but accurate picture of the burdens folks endure yet keep hidden in hopelessness or humiliation. Like an old worthless suitcase being drug around for years, it was time to let go and trust God with their future.

The sign out front was an invitation to anyone interested in joining us as we embarked on a new season dedicated to what God was doing. And so, having done all we could do, the doors opened, and we waited.

> *Now may He who supplies seed to the sower, and bread for food,*
> *supply and multiply the seed you have sown*
> *and increase the fruits of your righteousness.*
>
> **2 CORINTHIANS 9:10**

I will never forget the surreal feeling the morning we first opened The Crossing to the town of Nineveh in 2009. We weren't even sure if anyone would show up, but folks came. And they kept coming until we worshipped that Sunday with over one hundred people, mostly strangers.

While The Crossing started out with a hundred new acquaintances and a borrowed worship leader, through nothing but prayer and God's grace, by the second Sunday, we had a sanctuary filled with parishioners and our own worship team. The Crossing went on to have baptisms sixty-eight months in a row, and the altar has never been empty since that opening Sunday.

> *Fear not, for I have redeemed you; I have called you by your name; You are Mine.*
> **ISAIAH 43:1**

While driving to the church one morning to continue preparation for the church's opening, God began speaking "The Baggage" into my wife, Vicki's heart. Since it was before smart phones, she sat on the side of the road writing on napkins from her glove box. As she finished, an eagle soared across the sky. A gift from God? Who knows? But she will never forget that day.

Vicki and I always seem to complete one another in ministry and I've been so blessed that God joined us to journey through this life together. The following is a story she wrote, which speaks to me and so many others who have read it.

"THE BAGGAGE"

There she stood on the platform at the depot, with the baggage accumulated over her life piled all around her. She carefully kept the prettier bags out front for everyone to see. That was easy, for she had grown used to keeping them there. Those bags contained all the things that made her "good," things like good works and kindness. The ugly bags filled with sin she kept carefully tucked into the back of the pile, hidden from the world. That is where the Lord found her and accepted her—baggage and all.

And so, her journey began. If she had had a clue how far the train would carry her, who could say what she'd have chosen to do?

The first thing she noticed on her journey was that others weren't quite as comfortable with their ride as she was. She watched, amazed as depot after depot the people labored and struggled with their baggage. She didn't know what was in their suitcases, but when the Porter asked them to leave one behind, they would cling to the case and state, "I can't. I need this."

Still, from time to time, as they departed the station, she would notice a lone bag sitting on the platform, totally abandoned. It was never hard to identify who it belonged to, for settled in their seat, they either had serenity or they would anxiously glance back at the bag. Either way, the train never went back, for the cost would have been far too high.

Then, one day, the oddest thing started happening. To her horror, she noticed that her ugly bags were sitting right up front on the platform for the world to see. She rushed over to conceal them, to no avail. They just kept working their way to the front again. Glancing around, hoping no one noticed, to her distress, the Porter was approaching. With a sympathetic smile and the kindest eyes she'd ever seen, he asked, "Ma'am, may I take that bag and dispose of it for you?"

She stood there staring, thinking about how much she loved that bag. She was so accustomed to it that she could no longer remember life without it. Still, recalling the peaceful faces of those who had left their baggage, and relieved that he only requested one bag, she somehow found the strength to let it go. With trembling hands, she gave her bag to the Porter.

As the train pulled out of the station, she glanced back at the bag. It looked so shabby and ordinary that she wondered what all the fuss was about. She settled in with her lighter load and enjoyed the rhythm of the ride. And so, her journey went.

Station after station, bag after bag, the Porter would always make his request. Sometimes she would refuse, choosing instead to struggle back onto the train clutching her bag, but it always sat there accusing her until she came to hate that bag. It would never take many stops after the Porter's request till she left it behind with a sigh and a smile. From large and ugly to small and seemingly harmless, one by one, the baggage was surrendered to the patient Porter until she indeed traveled light.

As she stood one day on the platform, glancing down, she couldn't believe her eyes. All around her were bags, and they had her name on them! At first, she was filled with dread, thinking she had reclaimed her old baggage. But then she realized that she didn't recognize these bags; she didn't know what they contained. Curiously, she picked one up, only to find that it was light as a feather, and she wondered how long she had been carrying these bags without noticing.

Then, with the anticipation of opening a gift, she carefully opened the cases and sat there with tears of joy streaming down her face, for within the bags were the blessings of obedience. One bag was filled with joy, another with peace. There were bags of purpose, self-respect, faithfulness, and love. Bag after bag, she flung open the gifts until, kneeling there on that platform, she worshipped God in joyous abandon. She worshipped as only a woman could whose heart had been set free for its heavenly destiny.

Feeling a touch as soft as a lamb upon her shoulder, she turned her face upward, expecting to look into the gentle eyes of her friend, the Porter. Instead, she found herself alone — or was she? A single majestic eagle was soaring in the brightest blue sky.

There stood another at the depot, with the weight of her baggage all around her. As the glorious train pulled into the station, she knew that down the rail, she too would be asked to surrender her bags, for she had heard about the Porter. Without much concern, she decided to wait on the train that would never ask for surrendered baggage.

Do you know the Porter?

What baggage has He been patiently waiting for you to surrender?

Got It!

How has God enriched your understanding of truth through this stone?

In this last section I'm calling "*Dig Deeper!*", I hope you'll take the opportunity to do exactly that: to exhume hidden gems and veins of gold that perhaps were missed along the way. In my own studies on truth, I've found that the following verses brought a profound perspective that I think will enrich your relationship with God while fine-tuning your ability to filter out earthly noise and worldly deceptions.

After you have read the scripture in your own Bible (whatever version you're accustomed to), take a minute to write down its deeper meaning and how you can apply it to your daily life. Challenge yourself to reach higher by digging deeper, absent of ego, prejudice, or closemindedness. Open your heart to see clearly past falsehoods, as you ask the Holy Spirit to enable you.

"Men of corrupt minds, disapproved concerning the faith, but they will progress no further, for their folly will be manifest to all" (2 Timothy 3:8-9).

"Stand therefore, having girded your waist with truth, having put on the breastplate of righteousness, and having shod your feet with the preparation of the gospel of peace; above all, taking the shield of faith with which you will be able to quench all the fiery darts of the wicked one" (Ephesians 6:14-16).

"If we say that we have no sin, we deceive ourselves, and the truth is not in us" (1 John 1:8).

"My little children, let us not love in word or in tongue, but in deed and in truth" (1 John 3:18).

In the space below, record the new concepts you added to your foundation of Truth:

STONE #2

Obedience

Having confidence in your obedience, I write to you, knowing that you will do even more than I say.

PHILEMON 1:21

In all of the world's ancient histories—its anthology of heroic deeds, of self-sacrifice, and obedience to a higher calling—no single act of spectacular submission can rival Jesus's surrender to the cross. He was God, but He was also a man. He suffered the same pitfalls of flesh and blood, fears and foibles, that any human being does. Yet there is no one among us who will ever hang on a tree—to the point of death—for being perfect. In His deep love and obedience to the Father, He agreed to it, punished by gravity and nails and disdain, then died submissively before an audience of accusers.

In humility Jesus gave up His throne to wear a crown of thorns. He discarded His immaculate robes to wear a dingy garment of poverty. His language included everyone, and in speaking truth to those who were created through Him, He was understood by no one. What kind of God, in a universe where His glory is the only light shining, would consent to such a scheme?

One who reveres and defends the value of obedience.

As Adam and Eve defied God in their sinful disobedience, Jesus came to replace that act with perfect obedience. I pray that you and I, dear friend, will always strive to obey the Father, just as our Savior did. Because God is trustworthy, and He will never ask more of us than is humanly possible for us to handle.

No temptation has overtaken you except such as is common to man;
but God is faithful, who will not allow you to be tempted
beyond what you are able.
1 CORINTHIANS 10:13

God goes a step further to say that with temptation He will provide a way of escape that we are able to *bear it*. Strange that the way of "escape" isn't the complete removal of the temptation, but a means to endure it. I don't know about you, but this gives me a sense of relief. Just as God allowed Satan to tempt Job, He also gave Job the strength and perseverance to stay obedient to Him, and therefore withstood his tormentor. For Job's trouble, God restored everything that the enemy had stolen, then gave him even more.

God will reward our obedience because He is righteous and fair. That has never changed.

I don't believe the concept of obedience is too tricky for most Christians; we all know that we *should* obey God. However, I think the importance—the urgency of obedience and the degree of obedience expected by God—is underestimated. Nowhere in the Bible is obedience suggested, but insisted upon. Yes, obedience is essential to our relationship with the Lord.

When God took the Israelites out of Egypt, He led them along the farthest route into the wilderness, saying, "Lest perhaps the people change their minds when they see war, and return to Egypt" (Exodus 13:17). As long as God was doing all the giving, things moved right along. But as they journeyed further away from the familiar into the uncertain, and God began to reveal Himself to them, He came to expect more from them—He required obedience, born out of love and an elevated perspective of Him.

In the same way, Jesus, after revealing His true origin and identity with signs and wonders, said to those around Him, "If anyone desires to come after Me, let him deny himself, and take up his cross daily, and follow Me" (Luke 9:23).

The following poem paints the grim reality of rejecting Jesus, but the truth is that God never intended Hell for the creation He died to save. Every blessing and hardship on this earth is God's grace; an opportunity to come into a right relationship with the Lord.

Hell-bent is a mindset where Jesus has been considered and rejected, choosing "my way" instead.

God gives us all a choice to be the captain of our own ships or to allow Him to take the wheel. As you read, please consider your own life choices. May our epitaph read: I did it God's way!

"I Did it My Way"

Angels with mighty beating wings, powerful but lowly,
Sit at thy feet crying: Holy, Holy, Holy.
The world at your command, angels know their place
But far below stands the man, rebellion on his face.

Thinking he's in control, he shakes his fist at God and
says: I'll have my way; there will be no price to pay.
Surely in his wisdom, he can see—That were
the rain to stop, he'd simply cease to be.

Has he not noticed, when death comes to call, that
he can do nothing; no, nothing at all?
Has he not witnessed a crippling storm, Possessions,
life, livelihood taken and torn?

If he'd stop for a moment to acknowledge his plight
He'd go to his knees, seeking God with his might.
But no! He'll not bow; he thinks himself above.
He'll not humble himself, accepting God's love.

God will work and woo, but he'll never relent.
He's hardened his heart—you see, he's hell-bent.
So, with pity and love, God let go of his hand,
the self-controlled man fulfills his own plan.

Throughout his life, he will strive to gain worth
But never find peace; no, not on this earth.
The joy of surrender he'll never know,
In the blink of an eye to his grave, he will go.

In the pit of hell stands a statue so proud:

A haughty man with a beautiful face.
He rejected God; he did it his way
His tiny fist raised in its rightful place.

The inscription: I DID IT MY WAY!

VICKI TAYLOR

Obedience to God's truth is the only reliable evidence of a redeemed life.

Motivation regarding faith-based obedience can be put as plainly as this: our reason to obey God will be directly related to the truth we choose to live by—that is, our level of faith in that truth. The eleventh chapter in the Book of Hebrews is dedicated to those brave Israelites who lived "by faith" and were recognized for their extreme obedience.

The chapter begins with a familiar and much-repeated verse that Christians use when describing faith in its purest form:

> *Now faith is the substance of things hoped for,*
> *the evidence of things not seen.*
> **HEBREWS 11:1**

It means that as believers, we are sure that our prayers will be answered in tangible ways, although hope is the only thing we have to begin with. It means we're certain we will receive solid manifestations for our requests, though they are, at present, untouchable and unseen. This is faith.

The chapter goes on to examine a list of great acts of faith by ordinary people whose sole shared characteristic is that of faithful obedience. By faith Abel brought an offering to God superior to that of his brother, Cain, and God commended him for it. By faith Noah heeded the Lord's warning, and built a great ark, to the chagrin of his mocking neighbors. By faith Abraham left his home for a land he didn't know, but was promised to be an inheritance. He was promised a son, and though old and "as good as dead," by faith, he received that promise, which would eventually lead to as many descendants as the stars in the heavens.

So many more are mentioned in this letter: Enoch, Jacob, Moses, Rahab (a prostitute), Samson, David, Samuel, and the prophets. Just everyday people who were dedicated to their faith and obedience to their Maker. In this way, they are not so different from us, are they? Just regular folks going about their lives, while staying true to their North Star.

According to Hebrews 11:6, from where did they receive the strength, courage, and fortitude to obey God?

Specifically, what must a person believe when coming to God?

Now I'd like you to read Zechariah 7:4-7 and answer the following questions:

What question did God ask the people?

Even though they were obediently fasting, what charge did God make against them?

How does John 4:24 address the Zechariah passage?

Years ago, I heard God's call to obedience, and in the most terrifying way I could think of. Like many people do, I struggled severely with the fear of public speaking. Of course, this isn't rare. In fact, up to 75% of the population shares this common phobia. Some folks can break out into a cold sweat just thinking about getting up in front of a crowd. I was so intimidated by it, I felt certain that at some point, my secret would get out and I would be humiliated beyond recovery.

When I joined BSF Bible study with men much more learned than myself, my expectation was to do a lot of listening and very little talking. And so the journey of coming to know and love God's Word began.

Week after week, as I listened intently, God's Word transformed my heart until finally, I started sharing with my small group. The months passed and suddenly the year came to a close, which ended with, you guessed it, "sharing night." It was a great opportunity to stand and give testimony of how God's glory had touched us, and also articulate what we had learned that year. I remember that when the announcement was made, the only thought that raced through my mind was, "No, thank you!" And I meant it.

When that evening of sharing arrived, I showed up with my teeth on edge, even though I had no intention of speaking up. As men stood and began to paint emotional portraits of how the Lord had moved in them and their lives, I started to feel the presence of God. It was like a weight on my chest—not painful; more like a bear hug from someone that really, really loves you. At precisely that moment, I knew what He wanted: He was asking me to stand.

I wish I could say I happily threw caution out the window and gleefully stood and poured out my heart. Unfortunately, I can't tell you that, because I was too busy in the throes of a battle. I explained to God that I didn't know what to say. I wasn't eloquent or confident in my communication skills. Much to the contrary. I reminded Him of the challenges I had pronouncing words, and my fear that everyone would discover I was less educated—since I chose to take failing grades in school to avoid oral reports.

Still, God wouldn't resign from His all-consuming squeeze. Finally, without knowing how I got there, I was on my feet as my heart hammered away. Tearfully, I blurted out, "I love the Lord with all my heart," and quickly sat back down. In a handful of words, God had accomplished something miraculous in me. And I never saw it coming.

Well, I can tell you, that simple confession surprisingly touched the hearts of the men gathered, because they had just witnessed the agonizing yet thrilling act of obedience. Yet obedience pure and simple.

In my experience of walking with the Lord, I've found that He keeps His cards close to His vest. It's better that way. If I had known what He was planning for that night, I'm afraid I wouldn't have shown up. But God has a very soft touch. He is fully aware of our fears and phobias, and still manages to bring out the best in us, even if we forget that it lands directly at His feet.

It was in His power that the Israelites crossed through the Red Sea. It was His plan that brought Christ to earth to save His beloved wayward sheep. And it was His prodding that helped me over the hurdle of speaking out about Him in front of fellow believers. I just didn't realize that God intended me for a future ministry of public speaking and teaching.

But it wasn't long until I could see why He was doing it. My whispered words of love and devotion into His ear alone were not enough. My hours of thoughtful study in my home and silent meditation in my prayer closet wouldn't get the job done. When He designs a path uniquely for you—one of foundational stones that follow the map of His making—all we are required to do is take a single step, then another, and another.

As it was with me that particular night, it isn't necessary for you to have full knowledge of His plan—not even a glimpse. He simply wants your obedience. Does that act seem minor to you?

Break out your Bible and read Luke 16:10 and Matthew 25:23, then answer this question:

What do these verses say about "little" and "big" acts of obedience?

There are no "big" or "little" acts of obedience to God. There is simply obedience.

As you can see, there are no "big" or "little" acts of obedience with God. There is simply obedience. Keep this in mind the next time He asks you to do something outside of your comfortable wheelhouse.

> *Now it shall come to pass, if you diligently obey the voice of the Lord your God.*
> **DEUTERONOMY 28:1**

How important is the Holy Spirit in our ability to obey God? Would I, could I, have stood that night to speak without the power of the Spirit? Instead of staying frozen within my cocoon of self-doubt, I would go on to act far beyond what I was capable of—all in the power of the Holy Spirit.

In the Book of John, 14:15-17, Jesus tells us, "If you love Me, keep My commandments. And I will pray the Father, and He will give you another Helper, that He may abide with you forever—the Spirit of truth."

According to Ezekiel 36:27, what part does the Holy Spirit play in our power to obey Jesus?

The spark that ignites the Holy Spirit over our lives is obedience to His truth.

The spark that ignites the fire of the Holy Spirit over our lives is obedience to His truth. It seems a simple ask, in theory. Do what God tells you to do, based on His truth, and reap the rewards—that is the power of the Holy Spirit. Why on earth would we pass up such a gift? We can only assume that our autopilot has no off switch. Human will is a stern creature of habit, and our personal delights seem to overshadow God's truth and love for us at every turn.

Does the thought of God testing your faith intimidate you? Explain.

_____

_____

_____

No level of interaction with God should make you fearful. Some of the best tests with God are failed tests due to their humbling outcome. They show us our tremendous need to stay under the shadow of His wing. On the other hand, a passed test can cause our hearts to soar, filling us with boldness and confidence in Him. That's powerful too! Every Christian should wish for both—failure for humility and victory for reenergized faith.

We need never fear our God who loves us.

Still, there are things to remember about testing: to praise God in the process, and to love Him as He deems us worthy of testing. If we keep our eyes open for the time of testing, we will inevitably become an "A" student!

Read Matthew 7:24-27 and ponder its significance before answering the following questions:

What does it say about the action of obedience; what does Jesus liken the obedient to?

What test came and in what form?

Why didn't the house of the wise man fall?

What does it say about the consequences of disobedience?

Without the testing of obedience, how can you have security in your foundation?

Now let's read Deuteronomy 8:2. Can you put yourself in the place of those weary wanderers? Now take a look at the questions below and let them sink in before answering.

Who led the Israelites through the wilderness? Why?

Who is leading you through this life, and how do you respond to your times of testing?

Every command to obedience is a test, and we answer in only one of two ways: obey or ignore.

As we continue to examine the inner-workings of obedience, I'd like you to read Acts 5:27-29, then answer the questions below:

What was Peter's response when instructed by the council not to teach the doctrine of Jesus?

How can we apply this to our command to share the gospel today?

Let's move on to a story that most of us heard as a child, but holds new meaning now that we're adults. It's the lesson of Jonah and his decision to disobey God. Read Jonah chapters 1-4 before moving on to the following questions.

1. Jonah believed God and still went in the other direction. Jonah's actions revealed that he valued his own opinion more than God's. What do your actions reveal?

2. Did Jonah's rebellion against God only affect himself or did it affect others as well?

3. How can you apply that answer to your own life?

4. What would have happened if Jonah had not relented (surrendered) and gone to Nineveh?

Obedience 55

5. How can you apply what happened to Jonah to your personal life?

6. How far was God willing to go to bring Jonah into submission?

When we look at the outcome of Jonah's disobedience, there are several things that stand out:

- Jonah's circumstances seemed to fit into his own plans. (1:1-3)

- Disobedience will always affect those around us. (1:6,16)

- Disobedience will take you further away from God's plan than you ever thought possible. Instead, relent, repent, and see what God does. (2:1-10)

- Even though Jonah was used by God, he simply went through the motions, never experiencing the joy of being in God's will. (3:5-10)

- Jonah was so self-centered and self-absorbed that he had lost sight of what God wanted. You can't be God-centered and disobedient at the same time. (4:1-3)

- God's desire is for us to have fellowship with Him. He gives us a chance to change our heart and mind. (Jonah 4:5-11)

When we consider all that Jonah went through to avoid God's plan for him, how can you apply the lesson of Jonah personally? How vital is obedience to God?

What began as a private battle between Jonah and God became a very public, humiliating ordeal that put the men around him in danger. However, watching the struggle between him and God convinced those men of God's power—God took Jonah's negative act of disobedience and turned it into a positive. "But as for you, you meant evil against me; but God meant it for good, in order to bring it about as it is this day" (Genesis 50:20).

Disobedience took Jonah to the literal depths of despair, but God, in His mercy, met him there. Jonah's story ends with God still working to change Jonah's heart. In Matthew 12:40-41, Jesus acknowledges the effectiveness of Jonah's witness to Nineveh yet never mentions his petulant fits. That's God in His kindness and mercy—never allowing our weaknesses to outshine His strength.

As far as the east is from the west, so far has He
removed our transgressions from us.
PSALM 103:12

I remember a particular test regarding my own obedience; one that has stuck with me ever since.

It was a lovely August morning when I was on a jobsite for my own business, Taylor Door, when the phone rang and my test abruptly began. On the other end was the church from which we bought the building that housed The Crossing. We were three years into growing our congregation, and it was progressing just as I had hoped it would. I felt so proud of what God was accomplishing. The bills were getting paid, our church family was happy and well fed (so to speak), and everything was going great.

Unbelievably, the folks we purchased the building from said they were calling in the loan, needing the funds for another project. I couldn't believe it. How could God let this happen? What on earth was He doing, and where was I going to find someone who would loan a new church $300,000?

Suddenly, all kinds of thoughts rushed through my mind as I contemplated how to manage the problem: How much could I mortgage my house for? Was there someone at The Crossing who could contribute a large financial gift or loan? But before another gratuitous idea leaped into my brain, God gently *shouted*, "Don't you dare! The church will pay for itself in a way only I can do." And so I conceded, not knowing anything about His plan.

A short time later, I received another call, this time from a friend who lived in Florida. I shared our dilemma with him, and as good friends usually do, he stepped in, contacting someone he knew in Las Vegas. Now, stay with me. This person was aware of a believer residing in California who was eager to invest in Christian ventures. Before Vicki and I knew it, The Crossing had the money without anyone backing the loan—no credit check, no down payment—and with a suspiciously decent interest rate.

There it was, the map God used to bring the money full-circle: from Indiana to Florida, Florida to Vegas, Vegas to California, and back to a little church in Nineveh, Indiana.

It makes me laugh now (with the benefit of hindsight) at how easily God made this connect-the-dots design that brought enough money to us without me lifting a finger. There I was, ready to mortgage my house or ask another Christian for the finances to save something that wasn't even at risk at all. Only my lack of imagination coupled with my obedience to God left the door open for Him to orchestrate something only He could do—just as He had promised.

But God wasn't through with The Crossing yet. The church mortgage was paid off in the summer of 2022—just 12 years after its initial purchase—thanks to a generous $200,000 donation from an outside source. It's simply mind-boggling what the Lord can accomplish if we will only do what He tells us, no matter how confusing or useless it might appear. I've learned from experience to just step aside and let God do His thing. I guarantee you, it will knock your socks off!

> *Vindicate me, O Lord,*
> *For I have walked in my integrity.*
> *I have also trusted in the Lord;*
> *I shall not slip.*
> *Examine me, O Lord, and prove me;*
> *Try my mind and my heart.*
>
> **PSALM 26:1-2**

When we see what only God can do, it strengthens our faith to obey Him. As you remember the story of Jonah and his disobedience to God, can you think of a time when your own disobedience kept you from going straight to God's best?

Faith that can't be tested can't be trusted.

Remember how this Bible study came to be, with one man asking me to mentor him? How easy would it have been for this bi-vocational pastor to say, "I'm just too busy"? I would have missed the tremendous blessing of being in God's Word with these men, and *The Wilderness Way* would not exist. Obedience will be tested; how we respond will prove our faithfulness and trust in the One with the plan.

Another characteristic of obedience is blessings. What is a blessing if not recognizing God's undeserved goodness in our life? How do we always know what that looks like? When God makes a way where you saw no way. When the check you never saw coming appears in your mailbox. When God sends someone to show unexpected love and kindness. It's a part of His blessings that come when we unconditionally trust and obey Him.

But perhaps the greatest blessing of all is to walk in the power of obedience when used to further God's Kingdom.

When God awakened my sleeping heart to love Him, I was determined to give Him at least as much devotion as I had shown my business over the years. What some would call "radical obedience" would require many sacrifices. I refer to it as "what we're supposed to do." I knew well that my life could not stay the same and serve God. But there is no need to recount my acts of obedience; God knows. I've always known that it's impossible to out-give God.

> *I will make them and the places all
> around My hill a blessing; and I will cause showers
> to come down in their season; there shall
> be showers of blessing.*
>
> **EZEKIEL 34:26**

The Jordan River holds a great significance in my life; I founded The Crossing church on the concept of the Israelites crossing the Jordan into God's promised land—that is, the abundant life He had for His children. As of 2019, The Crossing has baptized over three hundred people. And I never could have imagined that God would take me to Israel, paid for by a young man whom I had prayed for and wrestled with over many years to lead into obedience. Indeed, an entire book could be written about his journey to Jesus through faithful obedience.

The byproduct of such faithfulness spills over to cover those people God chooses to bless.

Even though I was baptized at 12 years of age, in March of 2019, I found myself wading into the Jordan River to be baptized by the pastor of a megachurch (that shares the name The Crossing). Then, I helped him baptize many husbands and wives together. I cherish that memory more than anything the world could offer. Obedience equals blessings, and I want so badly for all who come to God to experience His blessings in limitless abundance!

Let's read Deuteronomy 28:1-6 and see what the Spirit tells us. According to these verses, what are the blessings of obedience, and what would you equate them to in today's world?

_____

_____

_____

What does Luke 11:28 say about obedience?

_____

_____

_____

When you compare Philippians 2:8 with Matthew 26:36-46, in what way did Jesus show obedience to His Father?

_____

_____

_____

Did Jesus find obedience easy?

Jesus paid the ultimate price in His commitment to obedience; however, we have the choice to obey. What does this tell us about God's character?

Since I was a young man in my 20's, I've owned a small commercial door business. My success plan for the first 20 years was hard work—to the point of insanity. I was determined to succeed in a world where small businesses came and went. Whatever it took, *and it took a lot*, I was willing to do. But as I watched time slip away while my boys grew up, I neglected personal time with them and my wife. There were countless phone calls where I begged customers for payment just to cover my own employees' payroll. Weeks would go by as I struggled to find the next project.

Life had become a cycle of physical labor, emotional stress, and miscellaneous stuff I couldn't control.

When I finally came to the end of myself and surrendered my life to Jesus, I turned all of that passion and determination toward Him, almost neglecting my own company, Taylor Door. What once was my pride and joy, soon became nothing more than a tool for surviving. Then, the most incredible thing happened—an epiphany or "ah-ha" moment that I would have to be blind not to see.

When I needed work, I would pray, and the phone would ring. When there was a bill to pay, I would pray, and a check would arrive. What I couldn't accomplish, Jesus could and did. My physical circumstances changed the minute my heart changed.

If truth is the base of our foundation, then obedience is the cement that holds the foundation together.

> *We do not look at the things which are seen, but at the things which are not seen. For the things which are seen are temporary,*
> *but the things which are not seen are eternal.*
>
> **2 CORINTHIANS 4:18**

Glancing back at Hebrews 11, we find folks who lived by faith, never dreaming of what the impact their obedience would mean in the future. What if Noah had not obeyed when God said, "Build an ark," or Abram if he had refused when God said, "Go"?

Hebrews 11:13 puts it this way: "These [people] all died in faith, not having received the promises, but having seen them afar off were assured of them, embraced them and confessed that they were strangers and pilgrims on the earth."

Likewise, there is no way of knowing what the impact of our obedience may have on the future. Obedience over time results in blessings, yet unseen!

As we read 1 John 2:3-6, according to these verses, what is the evidence of our claim to know Jesus?

_____

_____

_____

Obedience is the only reliable evidence of what we claim—our Christianity. It's what we do with that faith in Christ that will make all the difference, to ourselves and to those around us. Obedience is a choice, and it is in this choice we find God's favor. But it's so easy to ignore, drag our feet, or simply to forget to obey. That's why it should occupy our thoughts just as it was in the minds of those first pilgrims striving to reach the promised land.

When it doesn't seem essential to do God's will, choose obedience anyway. When it doesn't make sense to do God's will, choose obedience anyway. When it costs you more than you want to give, choose obedience anyway. When you simply don't want to, obey anyway.

For the Son of Man will come in the glory of His Father with His angels, and then He will reward each according to his works.

MATTHEW 16:27

Got It!

How has God enriched your understanding of obedience through this stone?

Now let's ***Dig Deeper!*** In the scriptures that follow, take a minute to meditate on their meaning, and write down what God is speaking to you about them. Don't rush, just sit in the presence of the Spirit and take in all that He has to reveal. Then move on to the next. It's these precious, still moments with His children that God treasures the most.

"And the world is passing away, and the lust of it; but he who does the will of God abides forever" (1 John 2:17).

"But be doers of the word, and not hearers only, deceiving yourselves" (James 1:22).

Obedience

"Jesus answered and said to him, 'If anyone loves Me, he will keep My word; and My Father will love him, and We will come to him and make Our home with him'" (John 14:23).

_____
_____
_____

In the space below, record what new concepts you added to your foundation of obedience by digging deeper:

_____
_____
_____

STONE #3

Glory

*When the Son of Man comes in His glory, and all
the holy angels with Him,
then He will sit on the throne of His glory.*

MATTHEW 25:31

I have been waiting eagerly to set this particular stone; however, without truth and obedience, it would be impossible to experience it completely and personally. It's like sitting down to a sumptuous meal without utensils. It may look delicious, but without the proper tools to take it in and enjoy its flavor and health benefits, it will stay on the plate, and you will miss the blessing. Its luxurious richness will remain a mystery.

While we may have a concept of the word "glory," explaining it is an entirely different matter. One cannot capture the beauty of God's glory with words. We must witness the majestic mountains or stand in awe of the roaring sea to even begin to comprehend it. Such is the glory of God.

To say that God's glory is the manifestation of His presence is correct. We must experience God's presence firsthand to fully understand it. Like the birth of a new baby, a walk through the woods on a crisp fall day, or gazing up at a star-filled sky, all these things proclaim the glory of God. But the way He chooses to reveal His glory is nearly irrelevant—the gift is that He does. And once He has, it is impossible to question His identity—the great I AM.

The biblical definition of glory is described as infinite beauty and majesty completed in pure perfection unattainable by man. The fact that God is without beginning or end is beyond our comprehension. Human minds cannot process that kind of enormity or omnipotence, but it's important that we continue to try. Never stop trying to recognize, appreciate, and worship the all-encompassing influences of God.

For my thoughts are not your thoughts,
Nor are your ways My ways," says the Lord.
"For as the heavens are higher than the earth,
So are My ways higher than your ways,
And My thoughts than your thoughts.

ISAIAH 55:8-9

Only God can reveal His glory to the common man, and from the beginning He chose to associate His glory with something we can grasp—light. From a burning bush glowing from a distance on Mount Zion, to the shock of light that blinded Saul (later called Paul) on his way to Damascus, God has begun great ministries through the light of His glory. "Let there be light" were the first words He ever spoke. Thus, His glory went from the invisible into the natural. He did this for our sake.

Consider the following verses: John 1:5, 1 John 1:5, 2 Corinthians 4:6, and Revelation 21:23 regarding God's Shekinah Glory.

In your own words, what is the Shekinah Glory?

The word *shekinah* is a Hebrew term meaning "dwelling." *Shekinah Glory* means "He caused to dwell," referring to the divine presence of God. In the Book of Exodus 40:34-35; 36-38, the Shekinah Glory is a symbol of God's acceptance of their work in building the tabernacle, and His presence therein, as well as His divine leading.

As the Israelites wandered in the desert after their exodus from Egypt, God's divine presence was manifest as a cloud during the day (Exodus 24:16-18; 33:9-10) and a pillar of smoke and fire by night (Exodus 13:20-22). He used these spectacles to guide them. It was something the Israelites had never seen before. What were the people to call this phenomenon? Their vocabulary had nothing to describe it, so sometimes they called it "the cloud," the "pillar of cloud," or "of the LORD." In other instances, "the glory" or "the radiance."

Today, we experience God's Shekinah Glory through His Holy Spirit. He still dwells among His people, giving them light, guidance, protection, and covering against the devil's assaults.

For anyone wishing to glorify God through their lives, they would do well to pray Moses's words to God:

> "If Your presence does not go with us, do not bring us up from here. For how then will it be known that Your people and I have found grace in Your sight, except You go with us?" And more directly, he said, "Please, show me Your glory" (excerpts from Exodus 33:15-16,18).

It is well and good that we should see His unrivaled creations and marvel at His imagination. But He is also quite aware that we are lost sheep needing tending to, so He reveals His glory to mankind to accomplish His purpose—to save and restore us to our original form. Perhaps that is why, as Christians, we feel overwhelmed by a gold-drenched sunrise, the perfectly laid pedals of an exquisite flower, or the seasons changing before our eyes. It is beyond our power, but easily done by our Lord.

When have you witnessed God's glory in such a way that it increased your faith?

_____

_____

_____

Many years ago (before The Crossing), we were on our last night of Vacation Bible School (VBS) in the church we were attending. Suddenly, God unleashed His Spirit. So many teens sought salvation that we could hardly find enough adults to pray with them. We didn't understand what was happening, only that it was a "God thing." We later baptized many of those young adults in our lake.

To this day, that memory is fixed as I recall God's glory coming down. I had never seen anything like it, and all I knew was that I wanted to live my life witnessing God's glory over and over again.

> *Arise, shine; for your light has come!*
> *And the glory of the Lord is risen upon you.*
>
> **ISAIAH 60:1**

Is God's glory always a profound, life-changing event? Perhaps it's only seen through the eyes of one who desires to witness God in all His power and majesty. This person will indeed see God's glory in countless things the world will never see.

To live as a Christian, satisfied without experiencing God's glory, is like standing just outside of heaven. The Christian who has caught a glimpse of God's glory will follow Him anywhere in search of more.

We must first desire God's way to recognize His glory.

Vicki recalls a time when she caught a glimpse of God's glory through the beauty of freshly fallen snow:

> As I made my way up to the barn to feed our eight horses after a newly fallen snow, the air held a stillness, as if the world had paused around me. The snow before me was blue, scattered with diamonds as it reflected the sun, covering all the ugliness of the barnyard. As the snow crunched underfoot and icy air filled my lungs, I felt a lightness of heart that turned to sheer joy at what I witnessed next. Hearing the thunder of horses at full gallop, I watched them burst into sight. Then, while they felt frisky from the newly fallen snow, I grabbed a front-row seat on a fence board and watched them play.
>
> I watched in delight as they ran, bucked, snorted, and pranced till, finally, the entire herd thundered past me into the barn. Following, I swallowed back a lump in my throat and worshipped God for allowing me the privilege of owning such magnificent creatures.
>
> To be near such power that the earth trembled as they passed and yet be able to walk up to one of them and rest my head against their powerful necks reminded me of Jesus. Having the power to destroy me, God displays His glory so that I might stand in delighted awe of all He is.
>
> As I stroked the velvety, snow-covered muzzle of my favorite mare and watched her steamy breath, tears streamed down my cheeks, and I whispered, "Let everything that has breath praise the LORD" (Psalm 150:6).

As I returned to the warmth of my home, I knew my heart had been changed forever by His glory. As most believers will attest, the soul that catches a glimpse of God's glory will never be the same.

The evidence of this change in Vicki is best described in a poem she wrote shortly after that very personal experience.

Snow

*The blue of morning's light
lies silent on the snow,
making earth clean and bright,
the filthy all aglow.*

*A hush fills the air
to still man's racing heart.
Creation's beauty shared,
God's gift He does impart.*

*White billows of love,
man's activity to cease,
Ordered from above
soft blankets of peace.*

*Sin like a crimson flood
Has earned just penalty,
Now covered by His precious blood,
His grace falls soft on me.*

*No wonder man is rapt
with the joys snow affords,
for it echoes God's great act
of love, the covering of our Lord.*

*For when He looks at me,
I'm clothed in glorious white,
my sins He does not see,
I'm perfect in His sight.*

VICKI TAYLOR

If we would open our eyes wide enough to see what God is doing all around us—in the Spirit and in the physical—what rewards await us, in gifts of beauty and grants of payment for our passage into His wondrous light.

> *Purge me with hyssop, and I shall be clean;*
> *Wash me, and I shall be whiter than snow.*
>
> **PSALM 51:7**

DESPERATE FOR GOD'S GLORY

The room in our windowless basement (we affectionately called "the cave") was where I retreated when my need for spiritual understanding overshadowed the world's noise and demands. It was 2004 when, through tears of anguish, I prayed the night long, asking God to release me to serve Him. It was there that God met me in startling fashion.

His glory flowed through me like lightning, and I began to speak with no personal requests or agenda, only to bring Him glory. The words that flooded tfrom my mouth were none I had chosen. It was blessed communion—spirit to Spirit—that brought a love language to my heart and spoken declarations of tenderness and reverent adoration.

From that moment on, everything in my life shifted. I would live the rest of my life for His glory, studying, praying, learning, and speaking for His glory. Later, I would preach for His glory. In those hours spent diligently seeking God, I knew I never wanted anything more than to live from glory to glory.

From that moment on, everything in my life shifted. I would live the rest of my life for His glory.

I was *desperate* for God's glory.

God gave Moses the task of leading God's people (approximately 2.4 million of them) to the promised land. While Moses had long died to himself, he so desperately wanted to complete his calling with excellence, bringing glory to God, that he knew it hinged on one thing—the presence of God.

Read Exodus 33:12-18 and answer the following questions:

What assurance did God give Moses? What repeated phrase do you find?

What did Moses ask of God, and how can we apply this to our ministries?

From verse 16, what argument did Moses make to persuade God?

It's an emotional conversation in which Moses virtually begs God to go with him when he is sent out to do God's will—to free His people. Moses understands that to represent God's glory, he must first have intimate knowledge of it before he can walk in it. And so it is with us. We must first choose God's way, drawing near to Him, in order to fulfill His glory through divine direction.

Let's read Exodus 33:19-23 before answering the question below.

What did God do for Moses, and why do you feel He granted Moses such a request?

Even after God said, "I will go with you," Moses reiterated how desperately he needed God to go with him and his cohorts to liberate the Israelites. He reminded God that the world was watching, and the only way for their lives to glorify Him was if He went with them! Once again, Moses pleaded, "please show me Your glory." How badly he needed the Lord, and how patient God was with him.

How badly do you want to see God's glory? How desperately do you want the watching world to see God's astonishing power? What amazing things do you suppose God could do through you if your greatest desire was to see His glory?

I can only imagine what it was like for Moses, hidden in the cleft of the rock, when the presence of God passed by. Through his close exchange with God, Moses was sufficiently prepared to lead His people out of 400 years of bondage. Though he didn't see God with his human eyes — lest he die — he was the recipient of that glory.

No matter how familiar or comfortable we become with our human means or spiritual gifts, we will never need less time with God.

After reading Exodus 34:29-35, explain what you learned via the questions below:

Why do you believe Moses's face glowed after spending time with God?

Why would Aaron and the people be afraid?

Why did Moses wear the veil?

_____

_____

_____

As we can see, God had already determined that His presence would go with His people, and that hasn't changed as He is always with His people today. It's our faith that believes we are never without Him, even though we cannot see Him. Still, His peace and the presence of His Holy Spirit continues to abide with us as we pursue His glory. Rest assured, He is with you!

> *Surely the Lord our God has shown us His glory and His greatness, and we have heard His voice from the midst of the fire.*
> **DEUTERONOMY 5:24**

REFLECTING GOD'S GLORY

There are some Christians who stand afar off, witnessing God's power in others, and longing to display it themselves. But instead of grabbing that first heavy stone of Truth, wrestling it into place, and then marching forward, they neglect the Stone of Obedience and dismiss God's glory as unattainable, reserved for a chosen few.

You, my friend, are loved and chosen by God for a purpose and a reason. Therefore, dare to cry out to Him as Moses did, "Show me Your glory." Just be ready to serve Him with all you have because His calling goes hand-in-hand with that glory.

The depth of your foundation will affect your ability to see and display God's glory throughout your life.

Before you say, "Well, that was Moses. What does that have to do with me?" read 2 Corinthians 3:7-18.

Once again, I ask: Why did Moses wear the veil?

What is our advantage, those of us with unveiled faces?

Now read John 16:5-15 and reflect on its meaning and message.

What is better than Jesus's physical presence?

How will you rely more fully on the Holy Spirit to teach you to serve and glorify God?

THE CROSSING'S MISSION STATEMENT

Our goal is to lead ordinary men, women, and children to embrace "Upward Journey" lives in Christ that results in Uncommon Christians, joyful and effective, demonstrating the power of God in their homes, church, and community.

When Vicki and I wrote the Mission and Vision statement for The Crossing, I assumed that as I poured out all of the passion in my heart, The Crossing would be uncommon in its desire and determination to follow God toward "Upward Journey" lives.

In the early years of our faith when God began to lay broken people at our feet, that should have given us a clue as to what God's plan was for The Crossing. It took fourteen years to fully realize that our church's mission was and is, in part, dedicated to the very broken. I thank God for all those who have helped me love those souls and show them the way to God's glory.

While we are all broken individuals, many desperately broken hearts and lives have come through the doors of The Crossing. Sadly, not every story has resulted in victory. However, we have learned to trust God and, more importantly, to recognize that our plans to glorify Him are not always His plans. Good ol' flesh and blood jumps in, only to get in the way of God's original design. Nevertheless, God will show His glory to His people, despite our best yet imperfect intentions.

Remember how God sent Jonah to the worst of the broken? Similarly, God sent The Crossing to the community of Nineveh, IN, to heal the broken. I quit wondering why we weren't like other churches when I understood God's calling for our church was different—and that's a good thing. It hasn't always been pretty, but in the end, it is a great privilege to walk closely with Jesus in order to love and serve all types of hurting people.

Those early days of my awakening faith were some of the best years of my life. The foundation God was building in me was something I loved and nurtured. I longed for opportunities to share Jesus, and that desire in me was satisfied in more ways than this book will allow to share. I'm grateful to God for the continued opportunities.

Like the opportunity that came about one Saturday morning at a carwash, of all places. My flashy yellow "Rumble Bee" truck had caught the attention of a group of soldiers who had just returned from their tour in Iraq. As they gathered round the bright, shiny machine, I felt the nudging of the Spirit, and talk turned to the lingering pain of war and the gracious love of God.

To my delight, we formed a circle in the parking lot at that carwash. With over a dozen uniformed soldiers united in spiritual solidarity, I prayed over them. That day, God's glory reached out and touched each of our hearts. I couldn't have planned it if I wanted to.

*A man's heart plans his way, but the Lord
directs his steps.*

PROVERBS 16:9

Let's read Luke 9:27-36 and describe the events that took place:

What was Peter's reaction to what he had witnessed?

While Peter was still speaking, what occurred, and what was the message?

As Peter pitched his idea about putting up three shelters for the visitors—Moses and Elijah, plus one for Jesus—he was interrupted by a cloud and a voice that suddenly enveloped them. Peter, John, and James must have been terrified when the voice said, "This is My beloved Son; hear Him!" It must have been traumatizing—the change in Jesus's face and clothing, the sudden appearance of Moses and the famous prophet, the cloud, the voice, and the abrupt disappearance of all of it. Can you imagine Peter standing there wondering *who* put *what* in the community well?

What we need to remember is, if we're not careful, just like Peter, we will attempt ways to glorify God that He never asked for or intended. However, as we listen and follow Him, He is faithful and will show us how to reflect His glory.

THE POWER OF GOD'S GLORY

Chapters 36-40 of Exodus describe the construction and equipping of the tabernacle "Tent of Meeting" in painstaking detail. First, the curtain, the ark of the covenant, the table, the lampstand, the altar of incense, the altar of burnt offering, and the basin for washing. When Moses had obediently done all God had asked, the most glorious thing happened.

Read Exodus 40:34-35 and describe what took place:

_____
_____
_____

Now think of the most awe-inspiring thing you have ever witnessed, then multiply that by 10,000. Next, imagine the experience of watching God's glory fill the tabernacle, as you envision that the same power is at work in you!

According to Ephesians 3:20-21, what can God's power do in you?

_____
_____
_____

Let's read Acts 4:13-16 before moving on to the next question.

What qualified Peter and John to heal people and display God's power?

_____
_____
_____

***God empowers ordinary men and
women to do extraordinary things.***

If you can't believe God uses ordinary folks to do extraordinary things, how can your life and ministry be for His glory and His alone? Expand your views of His goodness. God is gracious. He loves to share in His work and the blessings that come with it. He is a lover of children (that's us!) and dotes on them day and night. He is an amazing listener, to the extreme. And He lavishes His riches of all kinds on flawed creatures who barely acknowledge His astonishing generosity. How then could we doubt His desire to include us in the remarkable things He does?

The flipside of that coin is that we can misconceive our own abilities, making them grander than they really are. In all the universe, there is only one God, one Creator, one Alpha and Omega. Sometimes I chuckle when I think about how human beings give themselves credit when it is God's power behind the scenes doing all the heavy lifting.

> *Yours, O Lord, is the greatness, the power and the glory,*
> *the victory and the majesty; for all that is*
> *in heaven and in earth is yours; yours is the kingdom, O Lord,*
> *and you are exalted as head over all.*
> **1 CHRONICLES 29:11**

A few months into The Crossing, I began to pray about inviting folks to become members. Not long after that, while working in my barn, it hit me — an idea that would dramatize the connection between new parishioners and the church. I quickly went to work, cutting rope into three-foot-long pieces.

In our sanctuary hung a large, beautiful cross made of old barn wood. The following Sunday morning, I tied a long rope to the cross, which represented the church. I then invited the congregation to "tie on" as committed members. I wasn't sure how the idea would go over with people, so I was amazed as families stood in line until they were out the door, waiting to tie on. I watched as they approached the cross and slipped their piece of rope around the wooden beams, making sure their knot was good and tight. It was especially touching to watch parents help their children tie on.

And just like that, we were a church with members. What a God-glorifying Sunday morning it was! The memory has never faded, not one bit. I will always think of it as the day our family swelled, in warmth and commitment.

DON'T TOUCH IT!

What great responsibility comes with the temptation to touch the glory of God, even when it would grieve our spirit to do so. To understand how seriously God takes the offense, and how easy it is to "go there," read for yourself:

Numbers 20:6-13 reveals the consequences when we don't glorify God as we should.

Coming from the Lord's presence, what did God instruct Moses to do?

_____

_____

_____

What did he do?

_____

_____

_____

What was the consequence of his words and actions?

_____

_____

_____

If Moses touched God's glory, how vulnerable are we to do the same? It is a privilege and not a right to be of service to our Lord. May we always remember He is the "author and finisher of our faith" (Hebrews 12:2). It is "in Him we live and move and have our being" (Acts 17:28). What an honor for us to call Jesus a friend, but more so to give God credit when He is the architect of all things.

For My own sake, for My own sake, I will do it;
for how should My name be profaned?
And I will not give My glory to another.

ISAIAH 48:11

It makes me think of one of the first things we did when setting up The Crossing: we placed the phrase "To God be the glory" above the baptistry. For everyone who wades into the waters of baptism, there is a story of God's glory in hearing the gospel and receiving its Truth.

How blessed Vicki and I have been to be a part of the salvation experience and baptism of others, but all the glory is God's. Only Jesus saves. Let us all remain humble, taking pride in our lowliness, for we are merely the tools in His work shed. Our only proper response should be wonder—that He would trust us and allow us to serve Him in such a meaningful way.

Please examine Luke 9:46-48 and let it sink in before answering the following questions:

Why were Jesus's disciples arguing?

What was Jesus's response to their argument?

What are the dangers of allowing vanity to work its way into your calling?

Jesus perceived the pride in the hearts of His disciples. He knew that their arrogance could destroy their ministry. Sadly, there is conceit lurking in the church today that overrides the glory that belongs to God. It may be that the Lord will still use what works flawed people do, but He will never bless the doer, for "they have received their reward"—that is, the praise of people. From that point on, the work is done on human strength alone.

Touch His glory, and the power's gone.

Later, Jesus would give His disciples the power to heal the sick. Then folks became so astonished at what they were doing, that they would lay their sick in Peter's shadow for healing. Perhaps God has enabled you to do His work, and some of the recipients may not see the source of your power and end up praising you. Pray that as others pat you on the back, you give their admiration back to its rightful owner.

Jesus never called us to shine our light but to reflect His. What warning does Matthew 6:1 give us regarding our motivation for Christian service?

Bebo Norman sums it up very well through his song titled, *Nothing Without You*: "Take my time here on this earth, and let it glorify all You are worth; For I am nothing, I am nothing without You."

> *"When we encounter human praise or a manifestation of the presence of God's glory, we should be like signposts pointing all the glory back to God or like well-polished mirrors faithfully deflecting and reflecting God's glory rightfully back to Him."*
> **JOHN MAISEL**

Not unto us, O Lord, not unto us, but to Your name give glory,
because of Your mercy, because of Your truth.

PSALM 115:1

Got It!

How has God enriched your understanding of glory through this stone?

Now, let's *Dig Deeper!* Read the following verses and abide in the wisdom God imparts to you. Allow it to permeate your mind, your heart, your soul, before writing down your thoughts.

"Let them praise the name of the LORD, For His name alone is exalted; His glory is above the earth and heaven" (Psalm 148:13).

"Therefore, whether you eat or drink, or whatever you do, do all to the glory of God" (1 Corinthians 10:31).

"Arise, shine; for your light has come! And the glory of the Lord is risen upon you" (Isaiah 60:1).

In the space below, record what new concepts you added to your foundation of glory by digging deeper:

STONE #4

Love

And now abide faith, hope, love, these three; but the greatest of these is love.

1 CORINTHIANS 13:13

Love. Is there another word in this world that has been more abused, exhausted, twisted, perverted, or confused than love? It should come as no surprise since love is the greatest gift God has given us (Luke 10:27), having the potential to change the world if prominently placed in the foundation of the church and in our own hearts. As Christians, we were made in God's likeness. And if He is love (1 John 4:16), then it is an inherited trait that we carry with us, whether we realize it or not.

As we are made in the image of God's love, so Satan is here to make sure that we are distracted from our spiritual DNA thus disconnecting us from that love. The enemy would like nothing better than for us to neglect the greatest birthright we have.

C.S. Lewis broke love into four categories in his book *The Four Loves*. Understanding that all love is not created equal will be vital to accepting God's challenging command to love, found throughout His Word. We will look at four basic types of love to understand what love is and is not.

1. Storge (STOR-jay)

Family love is the affectionate bond between parents, children, and brothers and sisters. Examples in Scripture are Noah and his sons, the love of Jacob for his sons, and the intense love the sisters Martha and Mary had for their brother Lazarus. It's a love that says, "I love you because you're a part of me."

2. Philos

It is the love between friends. David and Jonathan epitomized this kind of love. For these two friends, their faith in God and trust in His will over their agenda drove them to a deep friendship. Paul and Timothy shared a deep love for God that bonded them in close friendship. It's a love that says, "I love you because you love me."

3. Eros

Eros love is physical, romantic love. Jacob loved Rachel and Abraham loved Sarah this way. The bride and groom in the Song of Solomon celebrate the gift of romantic love. It's a love that says, "I love you because you excite me."

4. Agape

It is the love of God, selfless and unconditional. Agape love is not primarily a matter of feeling but of will. The most extravagant example of this love is the sacrifice Jesus made on the cross for us and the willingness of God to give His one and only Son on our behalf. God's love commands us to love, whether we like it or not. It's a love that says, "I love you—period"! Without reason, without a return of love.

In an article written by Dr. Arthur W. Lindsey[2] about C.S. Lewis's thoughts on love, he includes the following directly from Lewis: "Love in the Christian sense, does not mean an emotion. It is a state not of feelings but of the will; that state of will which we have naturally about ourselves, and must learn to have about other people. It is good to have the feeling [of affection] as well, if they ever also play their part, so much the better."

The fact is, we cannot begin to comprehend God's love without His truth. We cannot hope to love as God commands without exercising obedience. And we cannot love God with devotion without first catching a glimpse of His glory. Each of the "stones" in this Bible study have a critical part to play as we strive ever closer to reaching and reflecting God's perfect love.

Love is mentioned an astounding 686 times in the Bible. The Gospel of John, sometimes referred to as the book of love, speaks of "love" 103 times. I often recommend this book as a starting place for new believers in order for them to recognize the importance of love as they seek to understand God.

---

2. www.cslewisinstitute.org/resources/c-s-lewis-on-love/

Until we comprehend that God is love, we will never truly know God.

*…being rooted and grounded in love,
[we] may be able to comprehend with all the saints what
is the width and length and depth and height—to know the love of Christ
which passes knowledge; that you may be filled with all
the fullness of God.*

EPHESIANS 3:17-19

I spent most of my adult life thinking I knew what love was. But it wasn't until I fully grasped the love of God that all other types of love became more natural, beautiful, and right, which gave them stronger meaning.

Agape love makes all other love less complicated.

Storge love, the love of family, gave me a sense of gratitude. When our family gathers together, I sit there and think, "Wow, God, look at them! You did all this!"

Philos love, the love between friends, makes me appreciate not what people can offer me, but I simply enjoy relationships on a deeper level.

Eros love causes me to look at my wife in adoration for her character and her love for God.

Recognizing the blessing of being loved and supported unconditionally is a feeling beyond words, and it all started with learning to love Vicki with agape love. The romantic love of this world is a cheap facsimile of the love God desires between man and woman.

Learn to love like Jesus and your life will hold together for eternity.

SEEING GOD IN THE DARK

Helen Keller once said, "I always knew He was there, but I didn't know His name." She had an innate understanding of God before she had the gift of language. How was that possible? Helen was blind and deaf before age two, unable to speak words she could not hear, let alone know what an actual word was. She lived a life of isolation, entirely in the dark, literally and figuratively. Helen had no means of communication. So, how could she have known God?

The best and most beautiful things in the world
Can't be seen or even touched. They must be
Felt with the heart.

HELEN KELLER

Later in life, Helen was mentored by an Episcopal priest, Phillips Brooks. Helen told him that she had always had an awareness of God even before she had any way of communicating with the outside world. Helen sensed God's presence in utter darkness but never felt completely alone. God's love for her was evident with her every step. When she finally had a way of understanding the name of God, she commented that He had been there all along.

In a short story written by Anna Nash titled, *The Time I Envied Helen Keller,* she recorded that Helen exclaimed, "Oh, that's His name! I didn't know He had a name."

There is no place God's love cannot reach. There is no silence He cannot break to reveal Himself. Without any outside influence to tell her who God was, Helen knew that "He Is," and that "He Is love."

Anna Nash was in awe that Helen Keller experienced God's pure love without the outside world's noise.

> *I always knew He was there,*
> *but I didn't know His name.*
>
> **HELEN KELLER**

When you tell children God loves them, they accept it naturally because they relate love to their parents. However, by the time that child is of an age to repent and surrender to Christ, all the experiences of human love throughout their life influences how they read God's Word. Reading "God is love" or "There is no darkness in Him" with the biblical accounts of God's wrath against mankind is difficult to reconcile within our minds without understanding God's compassionate nature.

Before we can exercise the powerful stone of love, we must first seek to grasp the heart of its source.

Let's read 1 John 4:8, 16 and answer the following question:

What repeated phrase appears in both verses?

_____

_____

_____

To say that "God is love" describes an attribute of God as well as who and what He is. Love is a core aspect of God's character, His Person. God's love is in no way in conflict with His holiness, righteousness, justice, or wrath. All God's attributes are in perfect harmony and will never cease to be anything less. Everything God does is loving, just as everything He does is just and right.

God's love is pure, without conditions or limits, and He has set that love upon mankind by the greatest of miracles. When God sets His will to love; there is no force in existence able to stop Him! God is the perfect parent; He will never give us anything but His best, and will fiercely protect His children. We would do well to place our tiny hand in His and allow Him to lead us like the small children we are.

Over the years as I've walked with the Lord, the following truths have become evident. They are simple yet unwavering, and I pray that they resonate with you. But if, by chance, they do not, then my prayer is that your relationship with God will strengthen as you spend more time with Him and in His Word. I offer these loving words of truth in hopes that you will repeat them often:

Jesus is the Parent; I am His child and He will never let me go.
He loves me so much, He gave His life to save mine.
He is the one with a clear vision for my life; I have learned that Father knows best.

He understands that I'm weak, and prone to unfaithfulness.
I don't have to be strong, perfect, or anything else to win His acceptance.
He doesn't condemn my failures, but patiently teaches me to do better.

He knows when I need encouragement or discipline.
When I need help, something or someone will appear to see to my needs.
Not because of anything I've done or deserve, but because I'm His child.

Read Romans 8:31-39, and reflect on what we have covered so far. Imagine the kind of love that the apostle Paul was talking about when he—with his brutal history of persecuting the early church and his hatred for Christians—felt when he wrote about God's unfailing love.

How do verses 31-32 prove that God is always with us?

What promise has He given us?

How would our attitudes differ if we remembered these two verses in every situation?

Define the word "intercession."

_____

_____

_____

Who or what shall separate us from the love of God?

_____

_____

_____

_____

When tribulation and suffering come upon us, what does verse 37 say about it?

_____

_____

_____

_____

If God is for us, who shall bring a charge against God's elect? Paul poses this question and others so that we may consider the unparalleled passion and power that is the birthright of being a child of God. Where do parents get their fierce sense of protection? Who could separate them from the love they have for their child? How much more can we believe that not even death, and certainly not Satan, can separate us from the love of Christ?

The word "persuaded" means to cause someone to believe through sound reasoning or argument.

When God created us for a relationship with Him, He could have easily fixed our love on Him. Why didn't He? Because down deep, He is a true romantic. It's much sweeter for us to be wooed by God, and for us to respond with a genuine heart of reciprocating love. In other words, it's our choice to love Him and to acknowledge and receive His love. And if we refuse to love Him back, then there's always a chance we can be *persuaded* down the road. He always leaves the door unlocked.

For I am persuaded that neither death nor life…
nor things present nor things to come… nor any other created thing,
shall be able to separate us from the love of God
which is in Christ Jesus our Lord.

ROMANS 8:38-39

To say that God loves everyone is true, but there is a distinction He makes in His love for His people. When He becomes our Lord, we become "more than conquerors." I fear that we have heard John 3:16 so often that we have lost our wonder at its truth. When we read it afresh, one can see what a miracle it paints in its words and meaning:

"For God so loved the world that He gave His only begotten Son, that whoever believes in Him should not perish but have everlasting life" (John 3:16).

Why does God love us? How can a perfectly pure being—untainted, incorruptible, morally unshakable, utterly virtuous God—feel anything but revulsion regarding us? As we already know, the substance He is, is love. I don't think He can hate us. He abhors our sin, but we are still His. We are made in His image, through Christ, and He remembers the archetype He started with, and like Him, it was perfect too.

I thank God for His long memory and tenaciousness to complete what He starts.

However, to live in the strength and confidence of His love, we must come to terms with God's agape love and mysterious words such as "elect" and "chosen." Our temptation to choose arrogance over humility is real. It is essential to understand that God's love for us has everything to do with His sovereign choice and purpose. Our response to this love has everything to do with us. We did nothing to deserve God's love, therefore, He will never cease to love us. The only appropriate response to God's unmerited love is "I'm not worthy!"

Woe is me, for I am undone!
Because I am a man of unclean lips.

ISAIAH 6:5

But God demonstrates His own love toward us, in that while we
were still sinners, Christ died for us.

ROMANS 5:8

Let's read Deuteronomy 7:6-8 and 1 Peter 2:9 and see how it adds to our growing knowledge of God's love.

What similarities do you find between God's description of Israel and Christians today?

_____
_____
_____

What point did God make about being "chosen," and why is that important to us?

_____
_____
_____

Why did God call us out of the darkness into His marvelous light?

_____
_____
_____

God's love is not dependent upon how He feels. It is His good will to love us.

I have said I don't like people, but I love them. When God began preparing me to become a pastor, I had to get past equating agape love with feelings. To help me along, God put two significant men in my life.

The first man was D.G. Morris, who taught me how to love people. D.G. was in his 70's and had pastored the same church for over 50 years. There wasn't much he hadn't seen or heard. For two years, every Friday morning before work, I'd drive 45 minutes to pick him up and head to Cracker Barrel, where everyone knew D.G. He seemed to know something about everyone. As he greeted folks with a "holy kiss," they felt loved, a rare gift in this world.

While we sat over breakfast, D.G. poured out wisdom gained over his five decades of perseverance. In affectionate humor, he would refer to people as "peckerwoods," a southern slang word for woodpeckers. If you have ever had a woodpecker camped in your backyard, you know what that sounds like, akin to a jackhammer!

Toward the end of our conversations, as he began to fade, I would have to practically carry him out of the restaurant. Still, I wanted to give back what I had learned from this uncommon person—a man who loved beyond what I had ever witnessed in my life. He simply took God's command to love others unconditionally to heart.

One of my sweetest memories is when wheelchair-bound D.G. visited The Crossing. Although my style was very different from his, he beamed at what God was doing there, and I knew he was proud of me. He died shortly after that.

The second man God put in my life taught me to love the church the way Christ loves the church. Dr. John Roszak has pastored Paisley Baptist Church in Florida for 30 years. I first met him while he was in town speaking at our church on other world religions, and our hearts quickly connected.

When I was rough around the edges (to say the least), and few pastors were willing to let me in, John opened his pulpit, and his church opened their hearts to me over and over. Their love and encouragement meant more to me than they will ever know.

No matter the circumstances, John never gets disillusioned, and won't allow me to, either. Through him, I learned how important it is for the church to love and reach out to help others. He believed in me, and I love him for it! When your eyes are on God instead of man, you see a man's potential.

CONVICTIONS

When we make it our priority to comprehend God's love, it will result in the Spirit's conviction that breaks the barrier of self-will, thus leading us to God's will.

> *I have been crucified with Christ; it is no longer I who live,*
> *but Christ lives in me, and the life which I now live in the flesh*
> *I live by faith in the Son of God, who loved*
> *me and gave Himself for me.*
>
> **GALATIANS 2:20**

When you read Daniel 6:7,10-11 along with Acts 7:54-60, ponder their interconnected meaning.

Why do you believe these men chose to honor God even amid extreme persecution?

_____

_____

_____

It is the natural inclination of people to follow their fervent convictions. Many soldiers have laid down their lives for their beliefs. Backing down was not an option. Their convictions defined who they were.

All but one of Jesus's disciples were martyred for their faith, and Peter went so far as to insist he be crucified upside down because he felt unworthy to die in the same way as his Lord.

In Philippians 1:21-25, what was the apostle Paul's dilemma?

_____

_____

_____

What does this say about his convictions?

How is it that divorce, addiction, pornography, and every other social problem the world faces, aren't nearly as common in the church? Focus on the Family attributes this to regular religious commitment and practice. People follow their convictions!

> *God cannot give us a happiness and peace*
> *apart from Himself, because it is not there.*
> *There is no such thing.*
>
> **C.S. LEWIS**

About 150 years ago, there was a great revival in Wales. As a result, many missionaries came to northeast India to spread the gospel. The region known as Assam was comprised of hundreds of tribes who were primitive, violent head-hunters.

Into these hostile and aggressive communities came a group of missionaries from the American Baptist Missions spreading the message of love, peace, and hope in Jesus Christ. Naturally, they were not welcomed. One minister succeeded in converting a man, his wife, and two children. This man's faith proved contagious, and many villagers began to accept Christianity.

Angry, the village chief summoned all the villagers. He then called the family who had first converted to renounce their faith publicly or face execution. Moved by the Holy Spirit, the man instantly composed a song that remains as powerful and convicting as it does today.

Emboldened by God's Spirit, he sang, "I have decided to follow Jesus. I have decided to follow Jesus. I have decided to follow Jesus. No turning back, no turning back."

Enraged at the man's refusal to submit, the chief ordered his archers to execute the two children by arrows. As both boys lay twitching on the floor, the chief asked, "You have lost both of your children, and you will lose your wife too. Will you deny your faith now?"

The man responded in continued song: "Though no one joins me, still I will follow. Though no one joins me, still I will follow. Though no one joins me, still I will follow. No turning back."

> *Your ears shall hear a word behind you, saying,*
> *"This is the way, walk in it."*
> **ISAIAH 30:21**

In a tunnel, about 30-40 feet beneath the Western Wall or "Wailing Wall" in Jerusalem, you will find an exposed, foundational stone. The stone supporting the wall's massive weight is the size of a semi-truck and weighs 40 tons. It reminds me of God's agape love: rock solid in truth, refusing to give up, enduring, resilient, dependable.

Wikipedia describes the Greek word *agape* as "the unconditional love that transcends and persists regardless of circumstance." Going beyond emotion, it is the highest form of love; the love of God.

In the book *William Barclay Insights, Love: What the Bible Tells Us About Christian Love*, it explains the noblest form of love as such: "Agape has to do with the mind. It is not simply an emotion that rises unbidden in our hearts; it is a principle by which we deliberately live. It is the kind of love we must have for all men—even our enemies (Matthew 5:44). The Christian must always act out of love, i.e., in the best interest of his fellow human being."

God has given us a detailed description of what agape love involves. Read 1 Corinthians 13:1-3 and answer the following questions:

The person with all the right words but lacks love is compared to what?

The person with extraordinary gifts but lacks love has what?

What does it profit someone who gives without love?

Countless times over the years, I've stood before couples just starting their journey as husband and wife. I've recited 1 Corinthians 13:4-8, knowing that if they go beyond the flowery words to embrace the deeper meaning, love will not fail them.

The exercise below is not reserved for married couples as we all have ample opportunity to practice God's love. Read the points connected to our love verses, and place a checkmark in the box next to each attribute(s) you feel you need God's help to do better.

- ☐ *Long-suffering:* Do you take a long time to get angry or do you have a short fuse? Do you justify anger?
- ☐ *Kindness:* Who are you least kind to or not apt to love? Is there any excuse to forego kindness?
- ☐ *Jealousy:* Are you prone to coveting or wishing you had what someone has? Do you feel slighted?
- ☐ *Boastfulness:* Do you ever find yourself bragging about something you're good at or what you've accomplished? How can God retain His glory in a braggart's heart?
- ☐ *Rudeness:* Do you walk past people at church or in your workplace without a smile or "good morning"? How's your tongue?

- ☐ *Selfishness:* Which is more important: your needs or the needs of others? Does your charity rest on mutual generosity?
- ☐ *Provoked:* Are you easily incited to argument or annoyed by a small miscommunication?
- ☐ *Rejoice in evil:* When you see injustice, does it sadden you or excite you? Does it urge you to join in?

Was that eye-opening, or were you aware of most of the answers already? It's uncomfortable to acknowledge the things we struggle with, and even painful when it's something that has gotten the better of us for a long time. But that's what the Holy Spirit is for; to help us mature in our faith and develop our moral fiber.

Now that we've covered the things we may fall short in, let's move on to things we can actively practice today!

Rejoices in truth: Love adores truth, and celebrates righteousness. Delight yourself in truth's victories, and find satisfaction in helping others do the same.

Bears all things: Love endures everything that happens, and is careful not to make the sins of another the subject of gossip or conversation. It chooses grace instead.

Believes all things: Love credits God's Word—all His truths and promises—and applies them to relationships, despite circumstances or feelings. Always be ready to believe the best in people.

Hopes all things: Love has confidence that it will succeed, even when there is no evidence left for believing it. It anticipates God's mercy and expects the best. Remember that no person or situation can slip beyond God's ability to change them or it.

Endures all things: Love bears up under persecutions and adversity. Love is hard, yet it silently perseveres whatever it must suffer.

Finally, *Love never fails:* No matter how impossible or unlikely, love will always win in the end.

How many families have been torn apart by five words: "I don't love you anymore"? And how could the outcome have been different had they chosen to practice agape love in their home? Eros love, when not reinforced by agape love, is fragile and tenuous. The fact is, everything on this earth will fail, but the love of God will carry us to heaven.

Read Matthew 22:37-40 and answer the following questions:

Are the words Jesus spoke to His audience suggestions or commands?

Will the second commandment be possible without establishing the first? Why or why not?

Agape love is not only God's love for His people, but through the power of the Spirit, He enables us to love Him right back in the same way.

When you read 2 Timothy 1:7, Galatians 5:22, and Ephesians 3:16-17, what do they have in common?

Lord, thank You for giving us a detailed description of agape love in action. Help us not to dismiss our unloving behavior, but bring our hearts into further submission to You. Enable us to see our need to depend on You for help. By the power of the Holy Spirit, we can and will conquer our fleshly body and emotional mind, in order to exercise the greatest gift of all—love. Amen.

If we live in the Spirit, let us also walk in the Spirit.
GALATIANS 5:25

The Crossing was only a few years old when a new family came into our church with three small children. We hardly had the time to know them or form the affectionate bond of philos love before tragedy struck.

It was a chilly November evening when I got the phone call. The couple's home was on fire with two small children trapped in the inferno. The mother managed to get her oldest child to safety, but sacrificed her life in the attempt to save the other two. Our church family stood in the cold winter air, together with their family, praying and comforting one another.

What followed next was a beautiful picture of agape love. The church quickly got busy, forming a support team for the father and his surviving daughter. Through fundraising efforts, our small faith community raised over $60k to help them rebuild their lives. That's love in action.

Through the display of God's love, the children's grandparents became believers and active church members. Mike, their grandfather, has since passed on, but we know exactly where he is. What a reunion he must have had with his grandkids who were waiting for him.

Their father, Chris, later met a widow at The Crossing who had a son of her own. They married and soon had a child. Chris and Melonie are a family with three lovely children who are integral to The Crossing.

Agape love brings out the best in people. I hope, after studying this section on what love is and is not, that you won't struggle with God's command to love. It's ok not to "feel" love for certain people as long as you "love" them as God loves them—through His eyes and in His strength. In the flesh, it's an impossible ask. But in the Spirit, it takes the burden off of our meager abilities, and places them onto God's all-encompassing goodness. Doesn't that make God's power of love remarkable?

God blessed my wife with a gift of encouraging words. I hope the following poem she wrote inspires you to love deeply and completely.

Love

How often do we bow to pray
Seeking direction to start our day?

We ask the Lord for wisdom and grace
His holy help here in this place.

We plea for strength from up above
But rarely request: I want to love.

For you see the great gift of caring
Won't be imparted; it comes from sharing.

Yes, all of us sinners down below
Wish to be zapped, but He says, "Go."

And never would He send us alone
For we have no power to love on our own.

Go to the world, be loving and kind
A mysterious miracle, you will find.

For when you do what He tells you to do
You're all about others, and He's all about you!

No greater joy in this world will you find
Than making a difference to a hurting mankind.

VICKI TAYLOR

In all the ways to describe love, to administer and receive love, to acknowledge and manifest love, there are just too many personal definitions that liquidate its true meaning. In this stone, we've categorized love four ways: *storge* (family), *philos* (friendship), *eros* (romantic), and *agape* (God's extravagant, selfless, unconditional love). Within the first three, we find love relying on our personal ability to feel. Only in the fourth are feelings swept aside to allow God's divine love that stands all on its own.

May we ask the Lord for the gift of agape love to work in us and through us each and every day.

Got It!

How has God enriched your understanding of love through this stone? Be as transparent as you can.

It's time to *Dig Deeper!* With so many Bible verses that mention love, let's just concentrate on the scriptures below. As you read them aloud or to yourself, meditate on their deeper meaning, through the eyes of God. Read the chapter and see in what context the verse is being used. Then think of ways to incorporate love into your everyday thought process. Write down what you can do to manifest Godly love—in prayer and in action.

"The Lord has appeared of old to me, *saying:* 'Yes, I have loved you with an everlasting love; Therefore, with lovingkindness I have drawn you'" (Jeremiah 31:3).

"If you love Me, keep My commandments" (John 14:15).

"But above all these things put on love, which is the bond of perfection" (Colossians 3:14).

In the space below, record what new concepts you added to your foundation of love by digging deeper:

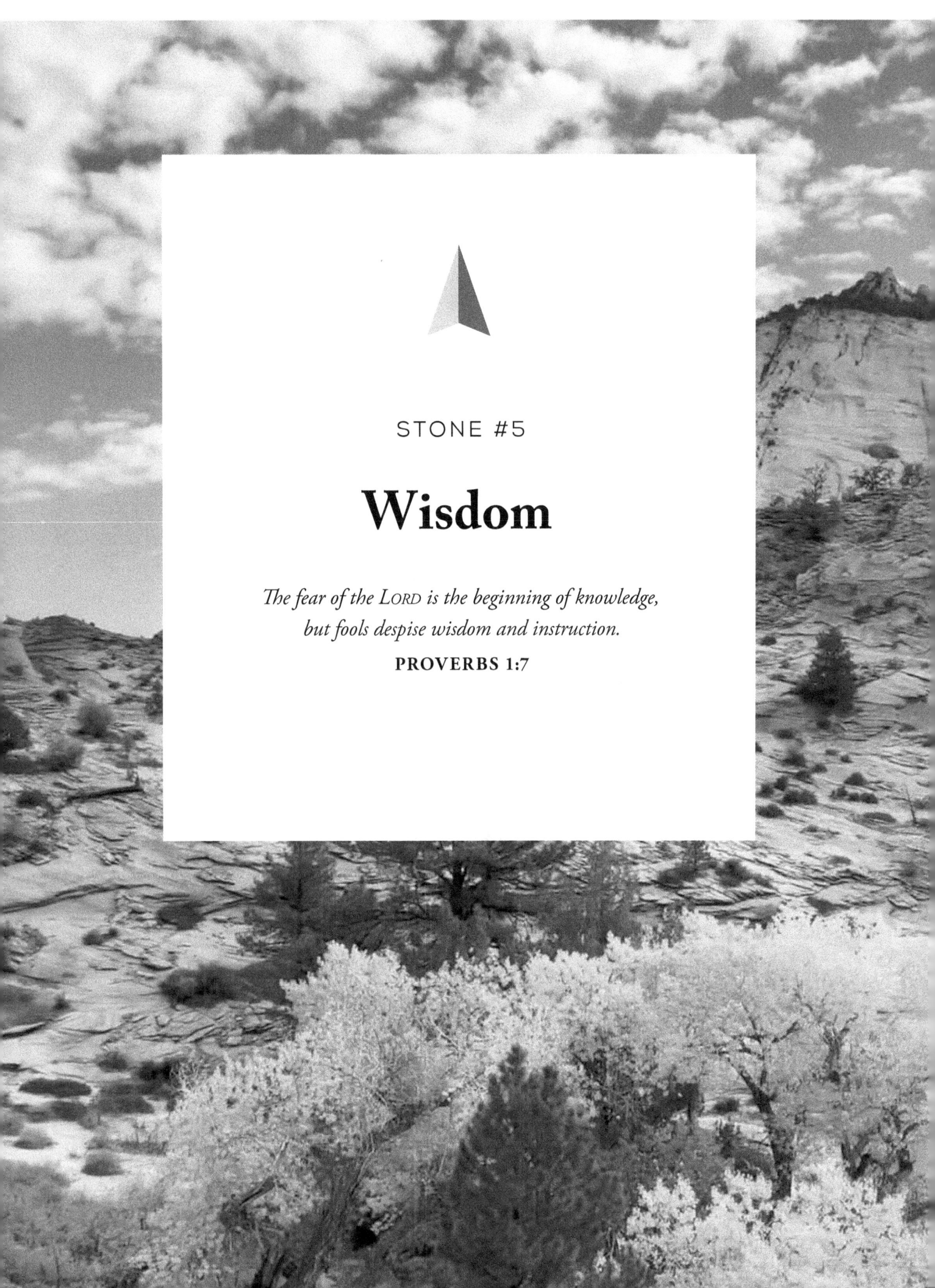

STONE #5

Wisdom

*The fear of the LORD is the beginning of knowledge,
but fools despise wisdom and instruction.*

PROVERBS 1:7

I think the stone of wisdom reverberated strongly in the heart of King Solomon as he writes about his personal search for life's meaning in the Book of Ecclesiastes. In his ardent quest for wisdom and knowledge, he tried everything—and I mean *everything*—to come to a final conclusion. With a blank check and a limitless imagination, Solomon began to explore.

He hit the books to digest all he could in the way of education and analysis. He devoted himself to reading texts on all human experience and inventions only to find that it came up short of his expectations. He indulged in pleasures of the flesh, spoiling himself in every erotic desire, but it left him cold and unsatisfied. Then Solomon put all his skills and talents to work, hoping that the plans, goals, and toil would result in fulfillment at what he had accomplished, to no avail.

He examined how time effected birth and death, planting and harvesting, tearing down and building up, mourning and celebrating, loving and hating, but nothing was mastered by time. He noted that in solitude and oppression he beheld the tears and anguish of friendless folks, the discomfort and isolation of those sequestered by life's ambitions and apathies. Laziness, greed, and envy were the byproducts of such a selfish condition, and Solomon grew sad at what he saw.

Even the riches accumulated in a lifetime became meaningless as he realized that as a man's hunger for wealth increased, his craving for more depleted his spirit. Evil was a companion to those who sought after the possessions of the world. As goods were produced and consumed, a person's growing appetite stole their happiness until they were robbed of sleep and rest.

And finally, when he was old in years and reflected on all he had seen and learned, King Solomon's heart was heavy. A common destiny fit for everyone was folly, as there were no moral men to be found.

At the end of his pursuit for the greater significance of living, he came to a single, startling determination. Everything under the sun is meaningless but this: "Fear God and keep His commandments, for this is man's all" (Ecclesiastes 12:13).

Wisdom steps out beyond the boundaries of knowledge to look deep into the life of Christ, for all else seems foolish without the gift of faith. Faith ultimately brings *truth* alive as *obedience* becomes our desire. God's *glory* leads to a deeper understanding of *love* as our heart begins to cry out to know more, hungry for *wisdom*. Through wisdom, a new beginning takes us far beyond our old mindset to a fresh realization of what is truly important.

With our stony foundation taking shape, we are ready to be led by the Holy Spirit through wisdom.

When I applied my heart to know wisdom and to see
the business that is done on earth, even though one sees
no sleep day or night, then I saw all the work of God…
For though a man labors to discover it, yet he will not find it;
moreover, though a wise man attempts to know it,
he will not be able to find it.
ECCLESIASTES 8:16-17

True wisdom is not man-made. If it were, it would be man's wisdom.

When considering biblical teaching by a pastor, what are the key things you look for? Are you more comfortable with a man who has graduated from seminary or perhaps even holds a doctorate in theology?

I will tell you, without a doubt, that I was the least likely to become a pastor. My education is minimal, and I have a specific learning disability that prevents me from hearing words correctly, resulting in poor spelling and mispronouncing words. One of the first principles God gave me while teaching a Sunday school class was, "It's not how much you know, but how much you love what you know." With that, you will grow.

That means I had to be willing to expose my weaknesses and insecurities to follow God unhindered. Remember the visual aid we used at The Crossing on opening day, "leave your baggage at the door"? I suspect that I sounded a lot like Moses when I felt God calling me to preach His Word. I shook my spiritual head and argued, "Lord, you know I can't spell. You know I'm not eloquent. Why on earth are you calling me to do this?" And while I was willing to attempt seminary, God assured me that it wasn't necessary. In my heart, I heard, "Through your limitations, I will be glorified."

*Now when they saw the boldness of Peter and John
and perceived that they were uneducated and untrained men, they marveled.
And they realized that they had been with Jesus.*
ACTS 4:13

Perhaps it's easier for me to depend on God because of my limitations, regularly asking for His wisdom and grace.

If you think you cannot comprehend the Bible and can only learn through schooling, then you are still looking within your own human abilities instead of walking by faith in the One who called you. I'm not against seminary in the least; nearly every person called into a full-time preaching ministry goes that route, as they should. I'm simply saying that God doesn't always work within our little predetermined box. He can and *does* impart wisdom into our hearts and minds that urges us to love Him and seek Him, regardless of additional academic education, natural talents, or human abilities.

If wisdom is understanding the world and how it works beyond common knowledge, then the world knows only one type of wisdom—gained through physical experience and knowledge. However, the brilliant physicist, Albert Einstein, admitted that "Wisdom is not a product of schooling but of the lifelong attempt to acquire it."

If God made foolishness the wisdom of this world, then that puts us all on the same learning curve! The common man marches through life without much concern for what comes after death, but wisdom marches forward, building a foundation on Jesus Christ crucified establishing our certain heavenly future.

The common man marches through life without much concern for what comes after death, but wisdom marches forward, building a foundation on Jesus Christ.

WISDOM VERSUS FOOLS

Since I've already admitted that my scholastic accomplishments are minimal compared to others in my field, I love reading quotes from people considered to be the most intelligent the world has to offer. In their brand of wisdom, I find a sense that my lack of schooling hasn't hurt me as much as I thought it did. Here are some entertaining thoughts you might appreciate:

"We are just an advanced breed of monkeys on a minor planet of a very average star. But we can understand the Universe. That makes us something very special."
STEPHEN HAWKING

"You shouldn't say 'animals' to distinguish between humans and non-humans. We are all animals."
PETER SINGER

"If the only prayer you ever say in your life is 'thank you,' it will be enough."
MEISTER ECKHART

"This is the true horror of religion. It allows perfectly decent and sane people to believe by the billions what only lunatics could believe on their own."
SAM HARRIS
(By his own admission, he is saying that billions of people believe in God. Why then would perfectly decent and sane people believe what is untrue?)

"Let's say a junkyard contains all the bits and pieces of a Boeing 747, dismembered and in disarray. A whirlwind happens to blow through the yard. What are the chances that a fully assembled 747, ready to fly, will be created through its passage?"
FRED HOYLE
(It's a great example of what it's like to believe everything in creation just happened.)

As you can see, it takes much more than university-level intelligence to find wisdom! Like King Solomon, the richest and most learned ruler of his time, we must believe in God above all, placing Him at the top of our priority list regarding study, dedication, and respect. If we do not, when His wisdom comes, we won't have the good sense not to touch the glory!

Vicki remembers the time she stood in an antique store one day with a group of women, deciding whether or not to buy a ridiculously expensive crystal bowl. As she stood staring at the bowl in her hands, all of a sudden, she became very unsettled, to the point of tears. All she could think of was, "is this as good as it gets?" God spoke wisdom into her heart that afternoon and her journey to the cross slowly began.

Although she had little head-knowledge, she somehow knew deep down that she had been given godly wisdom, which made her hunger for more.

> *What comes into our minds when we think about God is*
> *the most important thing about us.*
> A.W. TOZER

GOD ALONE IS WISE

Perhaps the greatest misconception about God is that He is somewhat like man. God isn't who we think He is; He's who He says He is. The Bible says that we were made in His image (Genesis 1:27), however, our self-centeredness tells us that He reflects us instead of the other way around. On a good day—when we are feeling our spiritual best—we can almost glimpse His beauty and divinity "as through a mirror dimly" but it falls far short of who He is in all His spectacular splendor.

God isn't who we think He is;
He's who He says He is.

Let's look at four words exclusive to God to gain a proper view of God and man, three beginning with "Omni," which is a Latin word meaning "all."

1. God Is Omnipotent

All-powerful (potent). Since He has all the power in the universe at His command, the Lord God omnipotent can do one thing as easily as another—no matter how simple or impossible. All His acts are done without effort and His power is unlimited in every way. He expends no energy that must be replenished. His self-sufficiency makes it unnecessary for Him to look outside of Himself for anything.

God's power is without measure. He can achieve any task, at any time, in any way He chooses.

I'd like you to read Job 38:1-41 and 40:3-5 and answer the following questions:

Which verse challenged your thinking the most?

What was Job's reaction to God's sovereign power?

How do these verses change the way you perceive your own troubles?

2. God Is Omniscient

All-knowing. God encompasses all knowledge of the universe's past, present, and future. In the beginning, God created the world and everything in it, including knowledge. Psalm 147:4 (NIV) tells us, "He determines the number of the stars and calls them each by name." God not only knows how many stars are in the universe but knows each one personally. A study has put the number of stars at 70,000 million, or 70 followed by 22 zeros. And yet, God appreciates every one of them individually.

God's knowledge is perfect. The omniscience of God is complete. God does not continually learn but knows everything at once.

Read Isaiah 40:13-14 and examine how you perceive your own limited knowledge.

Who does God seek for counsel?

When praying, how often have you offered God advice?

3. God Is Omnipresent

All present. God is present everywhere at all times. The human mind classifies events along a sequential timeline, with specific and even incremental divisions for the past, present, and future. But God, who is eternal, is not limited by time or space. As Alpha (beginning) and Omega (end), He rules simultaneously over all of human history, beyond the physical limitations of any timeline.

God gave us time to measure our human experience in the world we live in. He has no such boundaries.

Read Jeremiah 23:23-24, and answer the questions below:

What does this teach us about God's relationship to time and space?

Can you remember a past event when God slowed down time to meet your limits?

4. God Is Sovereign

Supreme in authority. All things are under God's control. He is the uncontested owner and possessor of heaven and earth. We may be the caretakers of our physical and material domain, but God has ultimate jurisdiction to call the shots. No one or thing can overrule His license regarding influence and agency. No spiritual entity, no earthly activity, no human intervention can derail or thwart God's final word.

What does Colossians 1:16-17 add to the concept of God's sovereignty?

Who created "all things," and why were "all things" created?

How are "all things" sustained?

Do you ever wish that you could overrule a God choice or decision?

These four words describing our God, Omnipotence, Omniscient, Omnipresent, and Sovereign, sum up the magnitude of how big God truly is. That's why written into the vision statement for The Crossing is the goal to teach a high view of God. To grasp the infinite, self-sufficient, almighty God, and to see ourselves in comparison to Him, in order to build a solid foundation of faith.

On a recent trip to our old stomping grounds in Florida, it suddenly hit me that everyone who was my age (64 at the writing of this book) who lived there when I did in 1981 was now dead and buried. Every single one. When you think about our earthly calendar and our short time here, God's timeline can make us feel very small and insignificant, indeed.

One of my favorite songs by the band Third Day says, "These thousand hills roll ever on, the footprints of a mighty God. They bring me to my knees in praise, amazing love, and amazing grace." In the book of 2 Peter, the Apostle Peter writes, "Do not forget this one thing, that with the

Lord one day is as a thousand years, and a thousand years as one day" (3:8). Imagine, 1,000 years goes by, and to God, it's like a single afternoon.

Or you could think of it this way: Even if one person had 1,000 years to study the entire compilation of acquired human knowledge, it would only be a day's worth of God's intellect. His wisdom made the sun, moon, stars, galaxies, the entire cosmos, and multiverses beyond it. Through approximately 8.7 million living animal species on this planet alone, we begin to realize only a fraction of God's wisdom and knowledge can be comprehended by us here and now.

God is big!

> *And I set my heart to know wisdom and to know madness and folly.*
> *I perceived that this also is grasping for the wind.*
> **ECCLESIASTES 1:17**

We all have the desire to be wise. We seek and search out wisdom and knowledge of the things of this world, just as we saw King Solomon doing in Ecclesiastes. But Solomon discovered that wisdom "under the sun," apart from God, left him unfulfilled and discontented.

Let's read 1 Kings 3:5-13 and ponder the following questions:

What did Solomon ask God for?

_____

_____

Why did this please God?

_____

_____

What did God give Solomon in addition to wisdom?

Why do you think God would do this?

Now let's look at James 3:13-17 and answer the following:

What do these verses say about godly wisdom versus earthly wisdom?

In James 1:5-8, let's read a bit more about wisdom before answering the following questions:

How are we to receive wisdom?

What stipulations are there in receiving wisdom?

What do you think it means to be a "double-minded man"?

In short, wisdom falls apart without truth, and serves no purpose without love. And if obedience is not applied, its calling is worthless. Through truth, obedience, and love, we witness the glory of God through the wisdom He provides.

Earthly wisdom appeals to the senses and emotions. In contrast, the wisdom of God reflects Himself. While earthly wisdom says, "always follow your heart," godly wisdom tells us that "the heart is deceitful above all things" (Jeremiah 17:9).

What's the difference in earthly wisdom when stacked up against divine wisdom? Let's look.

EARTHLY WISDOM SAYS:	GODLY WISDOM SAYS:
Seeing is believing	Blessed are those who have not seen and yet believe
Love family and friends	Love everyone, including your enemies
There are many ways to God	There is only one way to God, Jesus Christ

Examine 1 Corinthians 1:18-25 and answer the questions:

How does God compare the wisdom of this world with godly wisdom?

What does it say about Jews and Gentiles when hearing the gospel message?

Why are they different?

Now read 1 Corinthians 2:10-14.

What part does the Holy Spirit play in gaining wisdom?

What is the result when someone without the Holy Spirit hears God's wisdom?

PRAY FOR WISDOM

Instead of telling God what you need, try asking Him for wisdom instead. Luke 11:11 asks, "If a son asks for bread from any father among you, will you give him a stone?" That's an upsetting image, isn't it? Unthinkable. So if we who are so prone to selfish motives and eager to fill our own plate, can still give away beautiful things to those we love, then the God of all with every amenity at His command surely has the wisdom to impart what is best for us.

Seek God's perspective in everything. How often He has taken me to Scripture and met me there. Every sermon I have ever preached has been given to me through prayer and the power of His Holy Spirit.

Years ago, before surrendering to Jesus, I avoided writing because I struggled to hear vowel sounds and spell correctly. Still, I somehow knew that God would do something miraculous as I began writing with Him each morning. Within ten years, I had filled 15 journals with spiritual wisdom whispered to me by God's Spirit. And I know it is God because of the numerous folks who have been touched by it.

If you have never experienced writing (journaling in your quiet time), I kindly challenge you to try it. Though I have no background or education in the literary arts, I have still known the joy of creating words so profound and wonderful, that they simply could not have been written by anyone but God. It's an intimate and thrilling part of the relationship He offers to those who seek Him.

Next time you go to pray, take your journal with you. You may be blown away by what will appear!

Earthly wisdom is doing what comes naturally. Godly wisdom is doing what the Holy Spirit compels us to do.
CHARLES STANLEY

Got It!

How has God enriched your understanding of wisdom through this stone?

_____
_____

Let's *Dig Deeper!* With each stone in *The Wilderness Way*, I pray that this section is not passed over. It is my invitation to you to extend your reach, going further into God's holy Bible, searching for new revelations that only His Spirit is able to give.

> *"For wisdom is a defense as money is a defense, but the excellence of knowledge is that wisdom gives life to those who have it."*
> **ECCLESIASTES 7:12**

> *"Therefore whoever hears these saying of Mine, and does them, I will liken him to a wise man who built his house on the rock."*
> **MATTHEW 7:24**

> *"The simple inherit folly, but the prudent are crowned with knowledge."*
> **PROVERBS 14:18**

In the space below, record what new concepts you added to your foundation of wisdom by digging deeper:

_____
_____
_____
_____

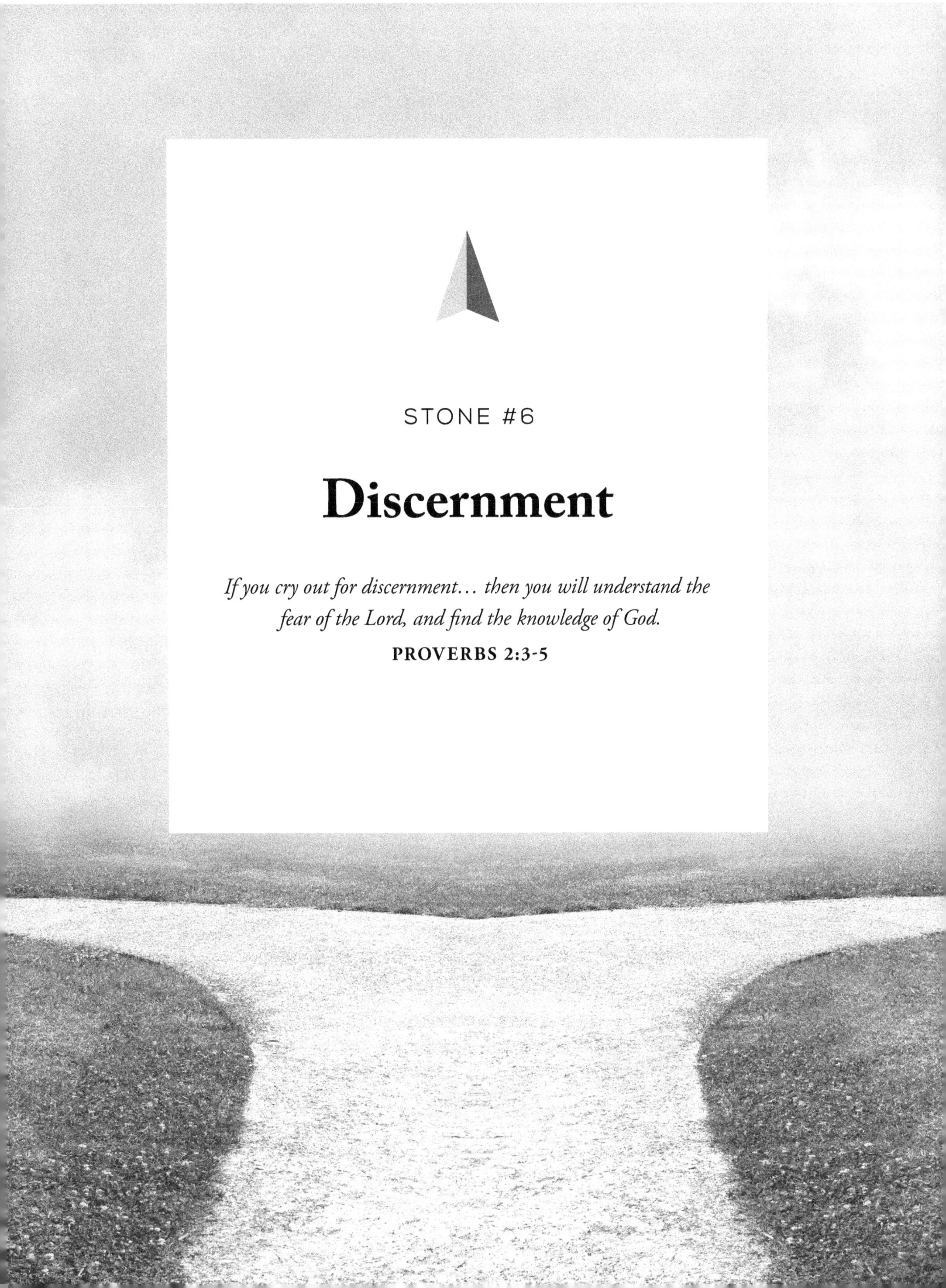

STONE #6

Discernment

If you cry out for discernment... then you will understand the fear of the Lord, and find the knowledge of God.

PROVERBS 2:3-5

In what now feels like a lifetime ago, John and Donna came into our lives to become our best friends. Perhaps because of the very special role they would play in our future faith, they were the instruments God used to lure us into attending church. The fact that they are just great people, I'm sure, also had a little something to do with it.

We had recently moved back to Indiana from Florida, and had bought two young, untrained horses. We quickly became overwhelmed with training them, and hired John and Donna for the job. Our first ride together was to "test" the horses, and we have ridden with them ever since. It didn't take long for us to notice that they were different from other couples. Their gentleness toward one another, their kindness toward others, and their willingness to go out of their way to help folks was nearly alien to me and Vicki. Little did we know that they were using our connection with horses for a deeper purpose.

Practicing good discernment, John and Donna understood that Vicki and I wouldn't respond well to being pressured or preached to. Instead, they simply loved us. Through watching them live out the gospel right in front of us, we followed them to church—then they followed us into ministry, becoming a loyal support to us and The Crossing throughout many years. Theirs is a quiet, mainly behind-the-scenes ministry, but their constant discerning willingness lends a hand in whatever God puts in their path.

John is known for saying "Uh-huh," which means "whatever you think." Discernment doesn't always offer solutions and answers, but it sometimes just lends an ear. Vicki jokes that she and Donna are best friends because she talks and Donna listens. Whatever the case, our dear friends always seem to discern what we need, when we need it, and are a great blessing to us.

Godly discernment can make for beautiful friendships.

> *I am your servant; give me understanding [discernment],*
> *that I may know your testimonies.*
> **PSALM 119:125**

Are you beginning to understand the order of the stones now? How can we begin to have good discernment without truth, obedience, glory, love, or wisdom? When you have a decision to make and are unsure what direction to take, how do you discern the right course of action? What about when you offer advice? Trying to exercise good discernment without deep consideration—a biblical understanding and commitment to—each of the prior stones will no doubt lead you to what *you* desire instead of where *God* desires to lead you.

Before I began building my spiritual foundation, I admit that my discernment was poor, at best. Discernment built on the flesh will always be established on self. A person cannot know godly discernment because they refuse to surrender their own desires instead of seeking God's perspective.

After years of drama and struggle—with what seemed like a weekly crisis—God finally got my attention. His unmistakable tap on the shoulder caused me to take a serious look at the stone of truth. When I relinquished myself to Him, His Word began to open up to me and with it His truth became more real. The more I learned and yielded to God's Word, the better my discernment developed and improved.

That's just the way it works.

In short, discernment is the ability to apply godly wisdom to any given circumstance. Having such a foundation gives you the much-needed understanding of God's nature, as well as the nature of man and evil.

What does Proverbs 2:10-11 tell us the key to discernment is?

How does having a discerning spirit benefit us?

Proverbs 15:21 offers a contrast between the wise and the foolish.

What is at the heart of folly?

What is the result of understanding?

The quality and integrity of the life you live shall, to a great degree, depend not upon your knowledge or physical or mental skills, but on your ability to discern what is right and good for you and your family. In the same way, godly discernment will never be found by asking the opinion of those around you.

What is the driving force of a decision you make when your "leanings" go against God's Word?

Do not be wise in your own eyes; fear the Lord and depart from evil.
It will be health to your flesh, and strength to your bones.

PROVERBS 3:7-8

The Devil doesn't care what side of the road you run off on, as long as you run off!

Without knowledge of God's Word, godly discernment is impossible. Many practices in today's world seem innocent. Even holy. But there are routines and rituals, disguised as God-centered and benevolent, that are pseudo-Christian spiritualism rooted in New Age or legalism.

In one instance, at The Crossing, I learned of a member who was practicing "sage smudging." Though I was pretty sure what that meant, I Googled the term. This is what I read: "How to Clear your Energy with Sage Smudging." It went on to elaborate that if you were feeling stuck in negative energy, or depressed, to try smudging. It is an ancient ceremony in which you burn *sacred* plants, such as sage, and the smoke will clear and bless the space.

As a Christian, this should cause your Holy Spirit warning bells to go off, as it is not scripturally sound. The Bible actually warns against it, telling us to avoid such behaviors. Deuteronomy 18:10-11 says, "There shall not be found among you anyone who makes his son or his daughter pass through the fire or one who practices witchcraft, or a soothsayer, or one who interprets omens, or a sorcerer, or one who conjures spells, or a medium, or spiritist, or one who calls up the dead."

By no means does it end there, as there are many more practices that can be placed under the same dark umbrella. Tarot cards, Rune stones, and crystal balls easily fit without the gambit of "the craft." The sure way of knowing if something is not of God is to search His Word—and listen to His truth.

Beloved, do not believe every spirit,
but test the spirits, whether they are of God;
because many false prophets have gone out into the world.

1 JOHN 4:1

Let us pray: "Lord, as we journey on, seeking Your truth, give us a spirit of discernment so that we may not stray to the left or to the right, but stay on the narrow path of righteousness. Amen."

Moving on, let's talk about the difference between knowing right from wrong, and applying good godly discernment to our lives.

Let's read 1 Kings 3:12 along with 1 Kings 11:1-4 and reflect on the following questions:

In 1 Kings 11:2, what was God's command and Solomon's response?

_____

_____

_____

How could the wisest man in the world have made such poor choices?

_____

_____

_____

What lesson is in it for us?

_____

_____

_____

God gave Solomon more wisdom than anyone before him, but his failure to "guard his heart" (Proverbs 4:23) affected his ability to have good discernment. When God gives us wisdom, it is up to us to choose to apply it. Otherwise, what good is wisdom without discernment?

Read Acts 16:16-18 and answer the questions below:

Why was the spirit giving testimony to support Paul's claims?

What was it about the slave girl's message that annoyed Paul?

Why didn't he cast out the demon at their first encounter?

If we've been paying attention at all as we travel through this life, we'll notice that things are not always as they seem. This makes it wise to be still, watch, and wait for divine discernment. Did the slave girl have a reputation as a fortune teller? Most likely, but maybe she'd had a change of heart. After all, the Apostle Paul taught repentance and change. And he ought to know!

Sometimes a wolf can genuinely become a sheep. Other times, maybe more often than not, they are disguised as sheep. I like to believe that Paul held back, choosing to watch and wait as he understood that what's down in the well always comes up in the bucket. Meaning, her true spirit was deep inside, somewhere, and eventually would reveal itself.

One thing is for sure, once Paul discerned she was riding on the coattails of God for her master's financial gain, he recognized the deceiving spirit and the danger it posed, and took action. The beauty of Paul's discernment was that the slave girl was set free from demon possession! What a lovely, valuable gift godly discernment is.

As a pastor, from time to time, I become aware of ungodly behavior within the church. I do all I can to allow grace, offer instruction, and pray in order to accomplish change. However, when I discern that I must deal with the situation, then I must. Just as Paul took action to protect the integrity of the gospel of Jesus Christ, so must the shepherds of the church preserve the health and safety of their flock.

Discernment is the application of godly wisdom, on display for God's glory.

In the multitude of words sin is not lacking, but he who restrains his lips is wise.
PROVERBS 10:19

Have you ever had someone come to you desperate for advice, but you let feelings or emotions take over? Later, as you considered God's perspective, you realized that your advice was not very good. As a result, you were of no help and perhaps even caused harm. It is Satan's goal to use those moments to defeat you, insinuating that your mouth would be better off shut.

But in the fog of condemnation for such a mistake, the Holy Spirit's conviction brings us to repentance, stronger knowledge, and dependence on God's Word. This, in turn, leads us to the right course of action next time—there is always a next time!

Discernment is not knowing the difference between right and wrong. It is knowing the difference between right and almost right.
CHARLES SPURGEON

A WEAK FOUNDATION WILL RESULT IN WEAK DISCERNMENT

In 1 Samuel, chapter 25, King David requested provisions for himself and his men from a wealthy man named Nabal who was known to be selfish, rude, and disrespectful. Nabal refused David's request, but before David could exact revenge, Nabal's wife intervened in the matter and provided the needed provisions herself.

Read from 1 Samuel 25:18-27, 32-35 and see the incredible difference good discernment can make.

In what ways did Abigail show godly discernment?

What was the result of her discernment?

What words did David use in verse 35 to encourage Abigail?

When have you been inspired to help someone through godly discernment?

Now let's examine James 1:5 and answer the question below:

How can we gain discernment?

_____
_____
_____

The discernment you share will only be as good as the discernment that's there. In other words, if you are lacking in God's Word, which feeds spiritual knowledge and discernment, then your human decision-making is all you have to rely on. If you're trusting yourself or others more than you're trusting God, I pray you will reconsider.

THE SPIRIT OF DISCERNMENT

For those contemplating how, when, and where to serve the Lord, discernment can become difficult. There are so many different ministries in which to channel your energy. Luke 10:2 reminds us that, "The harvest truly is great, but the laborers are few." Christians can easily find themselves in ministries that they were never cut out for. They end up spread too thin, or making ministry decisions based on personal preferences and/or comfort zones.

Faith is essential to our foundation, but what good is our faith if we are unwilling to express it through godly discernment? This will inevitably lead us back to what *we* have decided to do for God instead of what God has chosen for us.

I had determined myself to be an evangelist, going from church to church, and preaching God's Word. However, when God put an empty church building in my path and started opening doors, I had a decision to make. Through prayer and circumstance, I discerned God was calling me to establish The Crossing. Because of this, countless lives have been affected and changed through the ministry of this church. I thank God for the discernment that led me away from my will into His.

Now, read Hebrews 5:12-14 along with Philippians 1:9-10 and answer the following questions:

According to these verses, what is the way to godly discernment?

What was the Apostle Paul's specific prayer for the Philippians?

> *Trust in the Lord with all your heart,*
> *and lean not on your own understanding;*
> *In all your ways acknowledge Him,*
> *and He shall direct your paths.*
> **PROVERBS 3:5-6**

Years ago, Vicki and I picked up a woman hitchhiking who needed a ride home. During the drive, she told us she was ill then wove a despairing story where she needed $100 for an insurance premium before it canceled. When we arrived at the woman's house, I gave her my phone number and invited her to church; Vicki gave her the money. I later received a call from the woman's husband, informing us that we had financed her drug habit that day.

When dealing with brokenness, it's necessary, and sometimes critical, that we exercise spiritual discernment over human feelings. Vicki later recognized that she had ignored many warning signs in dealing with the woman, and felt terrible in that, far from helping, she had facilitated her addiction. She learned that serving others requires thoughtful, prayerful discernment. Since that day, until Vicki and I have all the information regarding the situation, we often use Acts 3:6 when dealing with requests for financial aid:

> "Then Peter said, 'Silver and gold I do not have, but what I do have I give you: In the name of Jesus Christ of Nazareth, rise up and walk.'"

The next time your heartstrings are hastily pulled in a direction that seems right, yet have the conviction of the Holy Spirit to withhold a "blessing" or aid, stop. Hold back, watch, and wait—for divine discernment that is sure to follow.

THE DISCERNING TONGUE

One of the hardest discernments is knowing when to speak or be silent. Wisdom surely does "cry out," and love holds a burning desire to see others apply biblical wisdom to their lives. However, while wisdom allows us to assess a situation correctly, discernment instructs us on how and when to address it. Ecclesiastes 3:7 tells us that there is a time to keep silent and a time to speak. But when? How?

Let's read Colossians 4:2-6 and answer the questions below:

What instruction did the Apostle Paul give in searching for discernment?

_____

_____

_____

How did Paul encourage his readers regarding their own words?

_____

_____

_____

Never before have there been more opportunities to voice our opinion. Blogs, chatrooms, and a battery of social media platforms with millions of followers have increased our need for God-given discernment.

To exercise good discernment in when to speak and when to keep silent, we can apply several Foundational Stones while asking these important questions:

- Am I speaking the truth in obedience to God or to myself?

- Is the act of loving others my motivation to speak?

- Have I humbly prayed, examining any plank that could be in my own eye?

- While it's tempting to blurt out wisdom, do I exercise godly self-control?

- Am I seeking to glorify God through my conversation or glorify myself?

All these factors will significantly influence the outcome of spoken words.

*Death and life are in the power of the tongue,
and those who love it will eat its fruit.*

PROVERBS 18:21

Yes, discernment is hard work! We gain discernment by exercising it, and as we do, our knowledge of God's Word grows. We learn to love others by living out our Christian lives with a sincere heart. Our ability to discern good from evil will also increase, along with our capability to discern the ministries God has for us. Suddenly, sound biblical advice will roll off our tongue, giving us the joy that Abigail experienced at having received godly discernment and exercising it.

While God does give the gift of discernment to those He calls to teach and preach, no one will find it who has not first built the foundation to recognize and exercise this gift. Keep walking with God by loving Him and His Word. Continue asking Him for spiritual discernment in your personal life as you serve His sheep. Never stop asking, and you will never stop receiving.

*For this reason we also, since the day we heard it, do not cease to pray for you,
and to ask that you may be filled with the knowledge of His will
in all wisdom and spiritual understanding; that you may walk
worthy of the Lord, fully pleasing Him, being fruitful in every good work
and increasing in the knowledge of God.*

COLOSSIANS 1:9-10

Got It!

How has God enriched your understanding of discernment through this stone?

It's time to *Dig Deeper!* As you've done with the prior Stones, read the scriptures listed below and pray how to apply them to your personal faith-walk. Journal about them in a separate notebook if the Lord leads, or use whatever *discerned* way of study the Spirit puts on your heart. I hope you will find comfort and encouragement in this study.

> *"By this you know the Spirit of God: Every spirit that confesses that Jesus Christ has come in the flesh is of God."*
>
> **1 JOHN 4:2**

> *"The manifestation of the Spirit is given to each one for the profit of all… to another the working of miracles, to another prophecy, to another discerning of spirits."*
>
> **1 CORINTHIANS 12:7,10**

> *"Folly is joy to him who is destitute of discernment, but a man of understanding walks uprightly."*
>
> **PROVERBS 15:21**

In the space below, record what new concepts you added to your foundation of discernment by digging deeper:

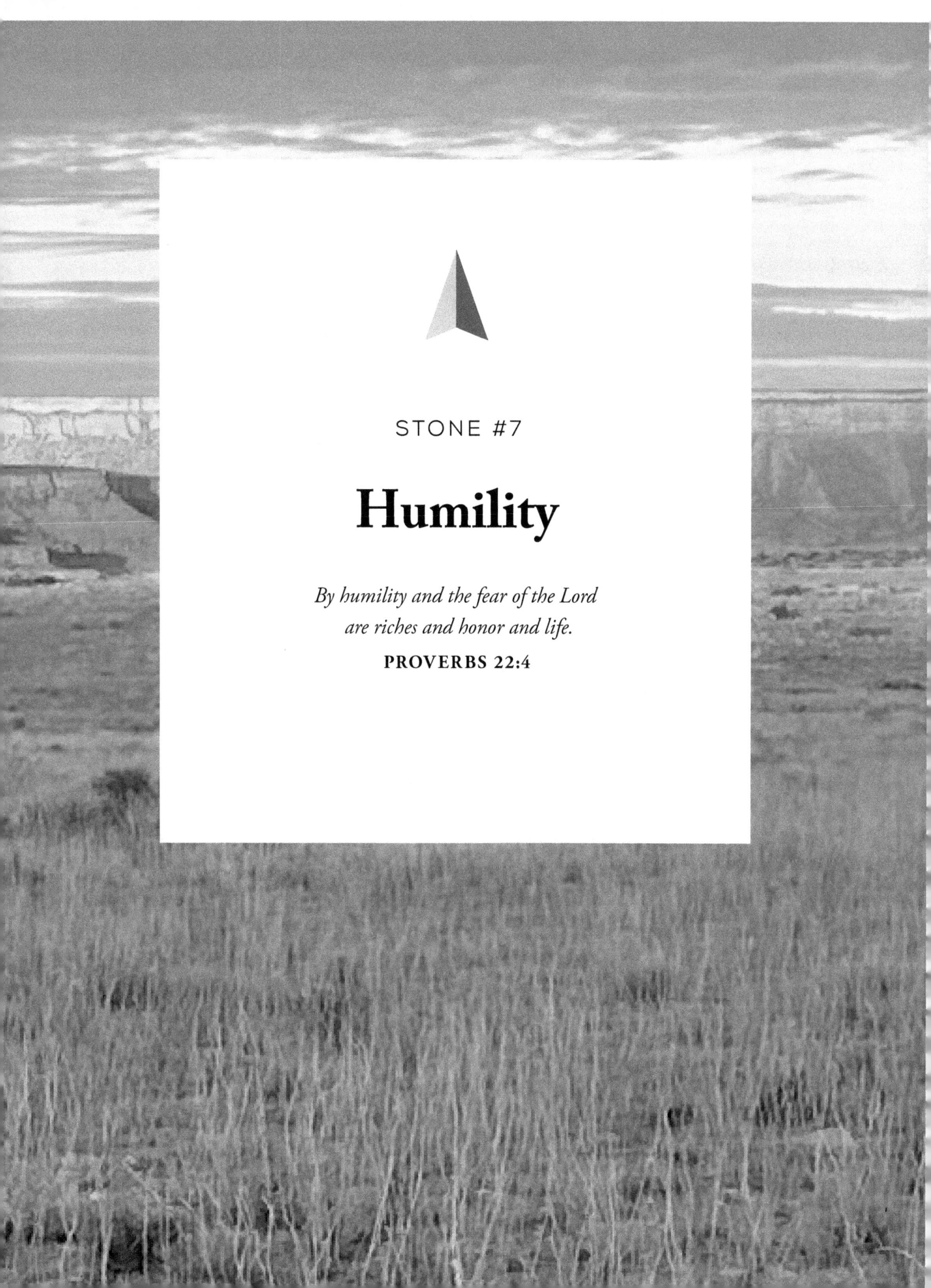

STONE #7

Humility

*By humility and the fear of the Lord
are riches and honor and life.*

PROVERBS 22:4

You, my dear friends, have made it halfway through *The Wilderness Way*! Whether revisiting these foundation stones as a reaffirmation of your faith, or gaining a new understanding of God's Word, I pray you are drawing closer to God every day.

This next stone asks the question: How comfortable are you with being humbled? If you're like most of us, it takes practice to really factor the concept into your walk with God. In complete transparency, I'd like to tell you a personal story that happened years ago when God offered me the opportunity to "humble myself in the sight of the Lord."

It was during an evening I decided to attend a BSF night, where members of my small group came together to share food and conversation. It was on this night God had made an appointment for me with humility, which came in the form of Alvin.

Wheelchair-bound with muscular dystrophy, Alvin had long since come to terms with humility, what I would consider an authority—even a PhD—on the subject. Who better to teach me? Alvin was completely reliant on people as he had only one working thumb, and depended on others to help him itch his nose, to eat, etc. Surprisingly, when I was asked to feed a man I barely knew, it brought on a flood of emotions—awkwardness, embarrassment, and even repulsion.

But as I started putting food in Alvin's mouth, humility washed over me and so began a bond and friendship that would further prepare me for future ministry. I would go on to spend many hours with Alvin at his nursing home, feeding him, talking with him, and hearing about all of the people he was reaching worldwide through his computer.

To my sadness, Alvin passed while I was out of town, but I cannot wait to see my dear friend in his glorified body in heaven. Alvin Koffman was a man of wisdom and sincere devotion to God. He taught me more about caring for the needs of others than any book could ever explain. I learned to look past a broken body into a person's heart thanks to Alvin, and God taught me humility and compassion through him.

I spent a few hours with him before Vicki and I left for a month in Florida. We both knew it would be the last moments of our time together, but we also understood that it wasn't "goodbye." My friend loved Jesus; he was a "soul winner" for Christ, to be sure. In this, I find peace and celebrate his victory of a race well run.

Toward the end, he lost the use of even his thumb, but I know that today, he is *walking* with his Savior.

My heart is full of joy for Alvin and I'm at peace with his passing. Not many folks will know the kind of humility he lived, but Alvin would tell you it was because of his disabilities that he came to know, love, and depend on Jesus. He thought of his time on earth as "a light and momentary affliction" compared to the joy that would be his for eternity.

He would often repeat a joke between us about how he would beat me to heaven and hold the pearly gates closed when I got there, but just for a *second*. I wouldn't be surprised if he does just that. And after we hug and laugh for a minute, he'll lead me to the heavenly banquet where I will marvel at our Lord's grace as I watch Alvin feed himself.

> *Therefore if there is any consolation in Christ, if any comfort of love,*
> *if any fellowship of the Spirit, if any affection and mercy,*
> *fulfill my joy be being like-minded, having the same love,*
> *being of one accord, of one mind.*
> **PHILIPPIANS 2:1-2**

The man who is humble before God has learned to humble himself before man.

Throughout the Bible, the characteristics of humility are present within those who hold not only knowledge of God, but a relationship with Him. Humility before God is a characteristic of those with a high view of God and a correct view of man. Humility knows its rightful place.

What would the characteristics be of someone who has a good grasp on the previous foundational stones but lacks humility? The Bible gives us a very detailed account.

Let's read Ezekiel 28:13-17 and learn more.

Who is it that these verses are describing?

_____

_____

_____

What was the final outcome—how did God deal with this lack of humility?

_____

_____

_____

Now take a look at Isaiah 14:12-14 to answer the following questions:

Write down 3 statements that prove pride took over, and what the result was.

_____

_____

_____

How many "I's" do you count, and what does this suggest?

As a side note, whenever I'm choosing favorite worship songs, written materials, or following spiritual leaders, it's my practice to watch out for how many "I's" are mentioned. If the words don't reflect humility, speak of dying to self, or come under submission to Jesus, I move on.

So, the most beautiful and blessed of all God's creations fell from heaven like a bolt of lightning (Luke 10:18) because he lacked humility — Satan. It would be easy to imagine a person with looks, talent, and position to let it go to his head. But I have a hard time reconciling an exquisite heavenly being, one so close in proximity to God and His majesty, to lose himself in ego. Such a cautionary tale, and one we can easily apply to ourselves.

In Satan's fury, he still seeks to pull mankind down with him. Pride ruined Satan, and perhaps that's why it is so detestable to God. We are to mirror the Lord, not His enemy — not our enemy. If we fail to recognize that power over us and fight it, we will also experience the truth — that pride goes before destruction (Proverbs 16:18).

God can use any man or woman who humbly depends on Jesus's power and purpose for their every spoken word and deed.

Rejoice in Christ Jesus, and have no confidence in the flesh.
PHILIPPIANS 3:3

THE HUMILITY OF JESUS CHRIST

To get a proper perspective on what humility is and is not, let's look at the Author of humility. Jesus made himself nothing by taking on the very nature of a servant. That means our Creator took off His royal robe and laid aside His awesome power and glory to become like us—human.

Kings are born in palaces, but Jesus was born in a stable designed and built for animals. He did this to show us the most effective model of humility. He humbled Himself by becoming obedient to death—even death on a cross where thieves and criminals paid for the crimes they committed. It was the pinnacle of physical pain and social humiliation of its day, where nine-inch nails were driven through the holy hands of Jesus, with a sword in His side adding insult to injury.

Was Jesus the King? You bet He was. But remember that He laid aside His sovereignty when He humbled himself to become the Son of Man. Jesus could have stopped His crucifixion at any time, and resumed His seat in heaven. But in order to reconcile us to Himself, to God, He chose humility in the form of a broken man to conquer sin—our sin—once and for all.

Jesus on the cross is arguably the most widely recognized image there is. But I wonder how many Christians often choose to think about the hatred, agony, and disgrace He endured leading up to those legendary and celebrated words He uttered—"It is finished!"

I'd like you to read Philippians 2:5-9 and let it sink in before writing your answer.

List three ways Jesus modeled humility and what God's response was.

Now read Mark 3:4-5 with Matthew 23:12-16, 27 and answer the questions below:

Regarding these verses, would you describe Jesus's demeanor as passive or aggressive?

_____

_____

Why do you believe Jesus used such assertive language?

_____

_____

_____

From your knowledge of the Bible, how did the Pharisees react to Jesus's bold truth?

_____

_____

_____

Every attribute Jesus exhibited while on earth was in perfect harmony and unity with His power. His humility never diminished His depth, capability, or authority to do just as He pleased. But it was in His lower position that enabled Him to do what He did—show mercy on a merciless mankind.

> *He was oppressed and He was afflicted, yet He opened not His*
> *mouth;*
> *He was led as a lamb to the slaughter.*
> **ISAIAH 53:7**

My point is that humility is not necessarily passive, though much of the time it can appear that way. We know that God's righteous anger can be found throughout the Old Testament, due to the disobedience of the Nation of Israel. But Jesus's arrival would put an end to the revolving door of sin and Sabbath sacrifice. This isn't to say that God doesn't get angry still. It is even recorded that Jesus became angry on several occasions, once turning over the tables of the money changers in the Temple's marketplace (Matthew 21:12-13).

But we now have the great Intercessor who pleads our case to the Father, and has already taken the punishment for us though we don't deserve it. I'm quite certain that the hardened hearts of the Pharisees made Jesus terribly sad. You can almost picture Him looking around in frustration, wondering how it ever got to that point. The religious leaders and children of God had been praying for millennia to see their Savior come, but when He did, they disregarded His miracles and accused His teachings of being sacrilegious. Their own lack of humility and pompous arrogance kept their eyes shut and ears closed.

The Pharisees were at a loss as to what to do about Jesus. They couldn't intimidate Him, challenge Him with their pointed questions, or manipulate His own words to suit their purpose. He was unstoppable! It's an amazing ministry for one so humble.

Humans, on the other hand, are far easier to bend. Today's secular society causes some Christians to back away from taking a strong stand against sin. They sacrifice their boldness to keep the peace. But how Christlike is that? And what has been the result of our fading confidence and courageous faith?

In the end, there should be righteous anger within us, but it should always rely on proper motivation, focus, control, and longevity.

I've found that there is no area in the Christian life more tempting to choose pride than in confrontation. Maybe part of it is just being male. So I caution my fellow brothers in Christ to be careful and prayerful when standing for God's truth. Remember, to belittle or disrespect another human created in God's image, is never approved by God.

Let's consider the characteristics of humility in the checklist below:

- ☐ Humility is gentle, patient, slow to anger, and not argumentative.
- ☐ Humility desires no recognition or glory.
- ☐ Humility is correctable and teachable.

- ☐ Humility is always in pursuit of God.
- ☐ Humility is self-controlled.
- ☐ Humility is under submission to godly authority.
- ☐ Humility is submissive to the Holy Spirit.
- ☐ Humility is committed to serving the church.
- ☐ Humility ministers willingly—no position or task is beneath it.

Is there anything on our list that is a challenge for you? As we study God's Word on humility, keep returning to this checklist for personal application. Continue to seek the help of the Holy Spirit as you gain ground.

> *[Jesus] rose from supper and laid aside His garments, took a towel and girded Himself. After that, He poured water into a basin and began to wash the disciples' feet… "What I am doing you do not understand now, but you will know after this."*
> **JOHN 13:4-5,7**

THE PURPOSE OF HUMILITY

We will never experience the *purpose* of humility until we choose to recognize its importance. It is when we humble ourselves under the authority God has placed over us that we realize how small we are and how big He is.

What does Hebrews 13:7-8 and 17 tell us about submission to godly authority?

How can you know who to trust to lead you correctly?

Jesus Christ is the same yesterday, today, and forever, "for I am the Lord, I do not change" (Malachi 3:6). The direction He provides us through His Word does not alter according to popular culture. Sadly, today, spiritual leaders are often reluctant to approach church members to (lovingly) confront them about their personal sins or warn them of signs of backsliding. The fear of offending them—thus worsening the problem—causes them to look the other way. But I hope I can encourage those of you who might be struggling with this to gird yourself with humility and strength in order to meet this demand head-on. Remember, agape love addresses hard things.

To submit to godly authority means to recognize that we are appointed with the same godly authority to keep souls safe—ours and those of our flock. I admonish you to take the responsibility seriously, and patiently, prayerfully administer God's rebuke to convict and restore them.

Can you recall a time when you discounted the council of one cautioning you in godly authority?

What was the result?

Let's read 1 Peter 5:5-6 and reflect on the following questions:

According to these verses, to whom are we to show submission?

What comes to mind when you read "clothed with humility"?

To whom are you submitting when you accept the words of godly authority placed over you?

> *"Humility is not thinking less of yourself;*
> *it's thinking of yourself less."*
> **C.S. LEWIS**

THE POWER OF HUMILITY

Speaking from personal experience, I can say that it brings a pastor great joy when a sheep receives a rebuke in humility and submission, thus teaching them its underlying power. The fact is, we will always struggle to submit to God until we learn to submit to the earthly authorities He has put in place.

According to James 4:6-7, how does practicing humility affect Satan's ability to influence your life?

Now let's read Matthew 18:1-5 and consider its wisdom.

How did the disciples' question reflect the attitude of their hearts?

What do you believe it means to humble yourself as a child?

How does Matthew 23:11-12 add to the conversation of the power of humility?

Does this scripture motivate you to change?

What are some ways one can show humility in action?

Why do you believe humility holds such importance to our faith?

It's not about how much you know; it's about how much you love what you know.

This truth stands firm in our foundation today. If ever you cross over from being humbled by God's word to being proud of what you know, you are heading into the company of the Pharisees. Remember, the opposite of humility is pride, so naturally, no one wants to admit that they struggle with humility, and there lies the irony. However, if Jesus's disciples struggled with it and the Pharisees stumbled over it, we better heed the warning about it!

As we can see, humility does not mean weakness. Instead, it is the source of strength in our Christian walk. In light of this, you wouldn't think humility would be so hard for us. When we achieve it, it feels terrific knowing we are pleasing God. Yet when we fail, it barely makes a dent in our mental psyche, which proves we probably need to work on becoming more aware.

Vicki used to tell our children, "We can do this the easy way or the hard way, but it will get done either way!" I think she got that principle from God, knowing pride is the path to destruction. God would rather step in and humble us than have us take pride to our grave. God loves us enough to make us a better person, just what a good parent does.

> *"Every Christian has a choice between being humble or being humbled."*
> **CHARLES SPURGEON**

While we're on the subject of pride going before destruction (Proverbs 16:18), the very same can be said about its opposite.

Humility devours pride, changing one's perspective of life, love, and hope.

The story I'm about to share is a stunning example of that very thing. I hope it speaks to you.

RAY

We took guardianship of my nephew, Ray, when he was thirteen. Like most teens, humility was not his strong suit. However, a battle of epic proportions between him and God began when he started to learn the Bible and heard the call to humble himself and surrender his life to Jesus. The years that followed were so intense that I began to fear he would choose death over submission. Every time Ray would sin, God was right there to convict him. He just couldn't get through his head that he couldn't do the things his friends were getting away with. He had been called by God; that was why God had put him in our home in the first place.

At seventeen, after years of continual drama, Ray chose to leave our home's shelter, safety, and comfort. From age seventeen to twenty-two, Ray was in jail twenty-six times and received three DUIs and two felonies. We were helpless to do anything but pray and wait.

He was under house arrest when we received his text one Sunday morning. In all caps: "I SURRENDERED." It remains the most precious text my wife has ever received. There were a few attempts to test God after that, but overall, the story of Ray is nothing less than a miracle. The last thing God meant for Ray was harm, but He insisted on his submission. There is no other way to Jesus.

Within two years, despite the felonies and his driving record, Ray had a nice car and a good job as an electrician. God has since given him a precious Christian wife and three beautiful children. Today, he owns a thriving business where humility serves him well, and he remains in church, serving the Lord.

That's the power of humility.

> *Seek the Lord, all you meek of the earth, who Have*
> *upheld His justice. Seek righteousness, seek humility.*
>
> **ZEPHANIAH 2:3**

Got It!

How has God enriched your understanding of humility through this stone?

_____

_____

_____

It's time to *Dig Deeper!* I hope that the additional scriptures below will light a fire in you to consider the deeper meanings of humility. Spend quality time with the Lord; listen to His opinion about your personal growth in humility, and abide in this powerful fruit of the Spirit.

> *"Humble yourselves in the sight of the Lord, and He will lift you up."*
>
> **JAMES 4:10**

> *"If there is any consolation in Christ, if any comfort*
> *of love, if any fellowship of the Spirit, if any affection*
> *and mercy, fulfill my joy by being like-minded."*
>
> **PHILIPPIANS 2:1-2**

> *"For whoever exalts himself will be humbled, and*
> *he who humbles himself will be exalted."*
>
> **LUKE 14:11**

In the space below, record what new concepts you added to your foundation of humility by digging deeper:

_____

_____

_____

_____

STONE #8

Self-Control

Where there is no revelation, the people cast off restraint;
But happy is he who keeps the law.

PROVERBS 29:18

Buddy, a huge "Moses" of a man with a heart as big as Texas, came into our lives many years ago. After two strokes and a heart attack, he finally came to the end of himself and surrendered his life to Christ. However, like many, he had serious consequences to overcome, including an addiction to painkillers.

To help him along his journey, Vicki and I moved him into a small apartment we had on our property. To show his gratitude, he helped around our horse farm whenever possible, and I could see that the very act of giving back fed his spirit. As he continued to struggle with self-control, several times he surrendered his bottle of pills, asking us to regulate them, as he couldn't be trusted. Sadly, within days, he would end up taking the bottle back.

Love, prayer, and patience were our only weapons against the steely grip drugs had over him, and as he grappled with his persistent habit, there were several times we thought we would have to ask him to leave. Thank God that never happened.

It was when Buddy began building his foundation of faith through the church and BSF Bible study, that he slowly but surely learned to depend on God for self-control. It was in this act of obedient surrender that he claimed victory over his life. Through Christ, Buddy went from a life of shame to a life of gain. He became drug-free, active in prison ministry, and achieved a relational ministry in his community, as those who knew him couldn't deny the complete change in him—from the inside out.

To my humility, Buddy always said that God told him to "look after Paul." As a grown man, I protested, but that never stopped him from doing what God asked of him. And he continued to support me in any way he could for more than twenty years. From bush-hogging (tractor-style mowing the fields), grading the driveway, and plowing snow, to helping with the horses, never a better friend has there been, bringing great joy to me as I watched him grow in his faith.

Buddy died unexpectedly while we were in Florida. Heartbroken, Vicki and I flew back to Indiana so that I could officiate the funeral. As the church filled to capacity, all I could think of was the extraordinary difference Jesus can make in a single life. Countless people stood to speak of his humility and the kindness he had shown them.

Had Buddy died the first year we met him, I'm afraid it would have been just one more story of a wasted life, excluding his service as a sergeant in the Marines as a gunny. Because of that, and so much more, Buddy was honored by representatives numerous Community organizations, Community service leaders, BSF, and Emmaus Walk, an organization that holds inspirational weekend retreats to know God better.

Through all Buddy had lost and gained, his humor had come out unscathed. Every now and then, he would send a text saying, "Won't be in church Sunday. In jail again. LOL." Buddy had his own brand of wisdom we lovingly called, "Buddyisms." One of my favorites: "I can't even control when I go to the bathroom. What makes me think I can control my own life?"

Now that's some homegrown wisdom! Oh, how I miss him.

Self-control is about yielding control to Christ for our good and His glory.

*Therefore, gird up the loins of your mind, be sober,
and rest your hope fully upon the grace that is to be brought
to you at the revelation of Jesus Christ.*

1 PETER 1:13

We live in a world filled with Self: self-ambitions, self-reliance, self-abilities, self-gratification, and yes, we even pride ourselves on self-control. However, when we surrender to Jesus, we are called to begin living under "new management." God's Word presents a brand-new life concept, as we are challenged to a life of faith, dying to self. Even the purpose of self-control changes as we seek to become more Christ-like instead of merely a good person.

Read Psalm 66:17-20 and apply it to your personal walk, then answer the questions below:

Which stones have we already discussed that was practiced by David when crying out to God?

When David wrote these words, was he mad, glad, venting? What was his spiritual posture?

What did God do in the end?

As we build our foundation on Christ more and more, life becomes about His truth, love, and wisdom. It pivots away from "all about me" toward "all about Him." Self-control is really relinquishing our personal ownership of the "building"—the temple that houses the Holy Spirit—for God to take full possession of it.

I used to base my self-control on my feelings, which rarely went well. As the owner of a commercial door business, nothing would set me off like walking onto a jobsite to work on doors, only to find them removed by floor installers or wet with paint. Any semblance of self-control flew out the *door* as expletives flew out of my mouth (please tell me you can relate, if only in hindsight).

But when I surrendered my life to Christ, I became aware that the same men I preached Jesus to on the jobsite were often the same who tempted me to lose control. I had no choice but to practice self-control or bring shame to the precious name of Jesus. Case in point…

Recently, I was on a jobsite and needed the elevator to transport me and my tools up one story. For reasons unknown to me at the time, the elevator operator didn't see it that way, and a little skirmish broke out.

There I was, *Pastor Paul*, trying to shove my workbench into the elevator with him pushing it back out. There was even a cheering squad shouting, "Let the old man in!" It wasn't until I was securely in the elevator going up—having gotten my way—that the Holy Spirit convicted me of losing self-control. I immediately grabbed my "opponent" in a bear hug and apologized, which was actually a blessing to us both. That's when he explained that his boss had been pressuring him to keep the elevator empty for supply runs, causing him a lot of stress. I was then able to speak to him about Jesus. I left the elevator shaking hands with him.

It's truly amazing what a little humility and kindness can accomplish when we surrender our ownership of what we want, and give it to the Lord of all. He can and will make something beautiful out of our messes.

But I discipline my body and bring it into subjection,
lest, when I have preached to others,
I myself should become disqualified.
1 CORINTHIANS 9:27

Self-gratification will always be at war with self-control. This comparative list makes the point:

SELF-GRATIFICATION	SELF-CONTROL
Anger feels good	Anger becomes a choice, not a spontaneous reaction
Selfishness wants its own way	Selflessness seeks what the Holy Spirit wants
Gives into temptation	Rebuffs temptation, putting it in its place
Feeds the ego	Builds humility and empathy
Disrupts God's plan	Allows God to maneuver
Foundation starts to crumble	Foundation holds solid

In the letter the Apostle Paul wrote to the new believers in Rome, he tells them that even he continues to struggle with self-control: "For what I will to do, that I do not practice; but what I hate, that I do" (Romans 7:15). He goes on to say that "nothing good" abides in his flesh, and evil still has its way with his own will. It's a stunning admission of failure, and still he transparently admits it to prove his point: That evil is a part of us now, and will always be until we are reunited with Christ.

He goes on to write to the Ephesians that "our struggle is not against flesh and blood," but it deals with the authorities in high places—dark angels and demons. But as with all hierarchies there is someone at the very top. In this case, God himself—that is, the Trinity. He alone has the final say in what transpires in our life.

Let's read Ephesians 6:12-18 to recall the armor that is at our disposal.

What are the six pieces of armor and what do they do?

Once we've put on the full armor of God, what does Paul tell us we should do then?

Why do you think it's important for us to keep praying for others?

When we place our life next to the life of Jesus, what do we see? He lived on earth thirty-three years, had a three-year ministry, and never once sinned. He didn't pursue financial wealth, personal celebrity, or place Himself above anyone else. Rather, He lowered Himself to wash the feet of His students.

In those three years of hard work bringing the gospel message to Israel, He was homeless, dressed in rags, and never complained about the miserable conditions. He traveled on foot in the sweltering heat and the bitter cold of the Middle East. And for the perceived blasphemy He preached, He was excommunicated by the religious leaders and shunned by the community in His hometown of Nazareth (Luke 4:28-29). Nothing about His life spent here was glamorous or self-seeking.

On His final night as a free man, He gathered His disciples to break bread only to announce that He would soon be sold out to the Romans (by one of them) and arrested. Can you imagine the horror they must have felt as the person they admittedly knew was God told them He was on the eve of His betrayal and ultimate death?

And in His final hours in the Garden of Gethsemane, when grief's shadow hung over Him, Jesus knelt down alone and prayed, still refusing to take control of His own destiny: "O My Father, if it is possible, let this cup pass from Me; nevertheless, not as I will, but as You will" (Matthew 26:39).

That prayer is, to this day, the Christian benchmark—a masterclass in humility and self-sacrifice.

> *"I do not seek My own will but the will of the Father who sent Me."*
> **JOHN 5:30**

> *"Did you not know that I must be about My Father's business?"*
> **LUKE 2:49**

The good news is that greater is He who is in me than He who is in the world (1 John 4:4). We may feel the uncomfortable pinch of temptation, but we don't have to let it get the better of us. It is in the power of God we can access His armor of protection. "Be strong in the Lord and in the power of His might" (Ephesians 6:10). It is the "helmet of salvation" that will insulate our mind from the whispers that appeal to our own willfulness.

> *It is the grandest life, 'having done all, to stand.'*
> **J.R. MILLER**

The concept of "self-control" implies a battle between a divided self. That's an easy idea for most folks to grasp. For example, we see a shiny new "toy" and say, "I want it!" Then we look at our finances, and the inner tug-of-war begins. It's like the image of our better angel sitting on one shoulder telling us to be good, and the little devil sitting on our other shoulder telling us to not listen.

Self produces desires—some we can satisfy, and others we should control. But how?

What does Luke 9:23-25 instruct us to do?

What is the outcome if we refuse?

What does it say our motivation should be?

There is so much to lose when we deny God's instruction to take up our cross daily and follow Jesus. He was the only human being who has ever lived a perfect life. No sin, no stumbles, no regrets. Only pure self-control. And don't think the devil didn't try to persuade Him to abandon His calling. For forty days in the desert Jesus was tempted to forget about God's plan, and to pursue earthly desires. But nothing could sway Him—not physical hunger, divine override, or worldly power would change His mind.

To every temptation, one response can sum up His warning to Satan: "You shall not tempt the Lord your God" (Matthew 4:7).

Let's read Galatians 5:16-25 and ponder the richness of its wisdom before answering the following questions:

What does it mean to walk in the Spirit and be led by the Spirit?

List at least three acts of a sinful nature:

What do we risk losing if we refuse to obey God's instruction?

What are the fruits of the Spirit?

As we walk confidently in the Spirit who dwells in us, He will provide all we need to thwart the enemy and our own self-gratification. What a blessing to know that we have been given so much—spiritual armor, the Word, His authority over the devil—which enables us to do all things through Christ who strengthens us (Philippians 4:13).

> *But thanks be to God, who gives us the victory through our Lord Jesus Christ.*
> **1 CORINTHIANS 15:57**

Now let's read 1 Corinthians 9:24-27 to establish how we should train ourselves.

What does it mean to be "temperate in all things"?

Would those close to you say that "temperate" is a word that describes you?

Where is God calling you to discipline your body and/or your mind?

This analogy of running a race is something we can all identify with. Whether watching the summer Olympics and those incredible athletes who appear to defy natural ability, or the race we run to meet a deadline at work, it seems that we're all racing to a finish line in one way or another. Hopefully, we train, mentally or physically work out, and we keep our eye on the prize to at last win the crown.

Is it any wonder that we lose sight of our invisible heavenly crown in a physical world that steals our attention, bombarding our human senses?

You remember my nephew, Ray. As a young teen, he loved to skateboard. One day, Vicki sat watching as he tried and tried again to perfect a trick, which turned out to be a painful undertaking, both emotionally and physically. He finally got so frustrated that he deliberately broke his board in half. His flesh overtook him until he suddenly cracked.

Vicki sat him down to gather his thoughts and feelings, and had him write Proverbs 25:28 one hundred times: "Whoever has no rule over his own spirit is like a city broken down, without walls." She understood that his lack of self-control had the potential to destroy his life. And indeed, it nearly did.

If your self-control is continually out of control, who then is really in control?

*Whoever has no rule over his spirit is like
a city broken down, without walls.*

UNDER CONSTRUCTION

Wouldn't it be wonderful to say, "I'm under new management," and never see the "old manager" lose control again? I've seen my share of tops blown for reasons that would quickly pass and have very little impact on tomorrow. Yet, tempers flare and go off, words are said that cannot be unsaid, actions on autopilot leave a permanent mark on someone who may not have deserved it. Unfortunately, we know it's not easy to reconstruct things, but what worthwhile thing comes easily? All we need is possible!

So how's your building project going so far? Would you say you are definitely under construction?

I'm getting ready to break ground to construct a new home, and I can assure you, it's not going to build itself. It's hard, time-consuming, thoughtful work that requires making daily decisions. And those decisions I make I will have to live with for a long time. Let's remember that it would be wise to give the diligence we apply to what "moth and rust will consume" to that which is eternal.

Read 2 Peter 1:5-8, and picture your own self-control before answering the questions below:

Define "virtue," and what part it plays in building self-control:

What virtues are ultimately added to one who has gained self-control?

What will be the outcome if we fail at building our self-control?

God is the perfect building partner, and will make something beautiful out of the one who is diligent in sticking to the blueprint. Yes, we are all projects in the making, but we are also the blemish-free wood in the Great Carpenter's hand, thanks to His Son—a specialist in human architecture.

For we are His workmanship, created in Christ Jesus for good works, which God prepared beforehand that we should walk in them.
EPHESIANS 2:10

Got It!

How has God enriched your understanding of self-control through this stone?

It's time to *Dig Deeper!* There's been a lot to consider, but now I hope you'll dig down a few more feet to really secure your building foundation. Read the following scriptures in a quiet time of peace and reflection. Study the words thoughtfully, prayerfully, and ask how you can apply them to your ongoing project.

"You are all sons of light and sons of the day. We are not of the night nor of darkness. Therefore let us not sleep, as others do, but let us watch and be sober."
1 THESSALONIANS 5:5-6

> *"[Be] hospitable, a lover of what is good, sober-minded, just, holy, self-controlled."*
>
> **TITUS 1:8**

> *"Put off, concerning your former conduct, the old man which grows corrupt according to the deceitful lusts."*
>
> **EPHESIANS 4:22**

In the space below, record what new concepts you added to your foundation of self-control by digging deeper:

_____

_____

_____

_____

STONE #9

Perseverance

Count it all joy when you fall into various trials, knowing that the testing of your faith produces patience.

JAMES 1:2-3

I'm not a quitter! At least that's what I thought until God took me on a fifteen-year journey that would bring me back home at the age of forty, beaten down and mentally bruised, but humbled. It was then that I was ready to hear His voice—much the wiser for my years in the wilderness.

I was twenty-five years old when I packed up my wife and two sons and headed for the land of milk and honey, aka Florida. With $300 to my name, I hung out my "Taylor Door" shingle and went to work. Over the next fifteen years, I would learn that people are not always honest and good, and that hard work and determination doesn't always guarantee success. I also found out that possessions don't always make a man happy. Rather, in some cases, they will leave him perpetually reaching for the next "shiny thing."

Oh, how I tried to persevere in life, but instead I learned that Jesus will patiently wait for us to come to the end of ourselves to find He who is worthy of our all, Jesus Christ. I'm thankful for those hard years in the wilderness that taught me that the most beautiful sight at the end of our wanderings is Jesus, waiting with open arms.

While owning a business can be stressful, it pales in comparison to being a pastor. Indeed, it is only through the Holy Spirit that I find the courage to persevere. Dealing with church disunity, counseling couples in marriage crisis, ministering to the sick and dying, managing betrayals, and battling the evil that whispers doubt in my ear, I come out victorious because of the calling of Christ and the help of His Holy Spirit.

Before I preached my first sermon at The Crossing, I sat at my church desk and prayed, not having a clue as to what the future would hold. I wasn't even sure I could write a sermon every week! I had to overcome countless doubts and fears. But as I prayed and leaned into God, I heard Him say to me, "Stay close, Paul. This church is Mine, not yours. Don't look at people. Look at Me. I've got you."

The next fourteen years at The Crossing would teach me the depth of true perseverance.

> *No temptation has overtaken you except such as is common to man; but God is faithful, who will not allow you to be tempted beyond what you are able… to bear.*
> **1 CORINTHIANS 10:13**

He goes on to say that He "will also make the way of escape, that you may be able to bear it." That's important. He doesn't say that He will remove the trial, or that we will "escape" it by leaving it behind. He says that He will give us all we need to bear (endure) it.

It reminds me of what Phillips Brooks writes: "Do not pray for easy lives. Pray to be stronger men. Don't pray for tasks equal to your powers. Pray for powers equal to your tasks. Then the doing of your work shall be no miracle, but *you* shall be the miracle." Therefore, my friend, I encourage you to run a race worthy of your strength in Christ.

We've all heard the story of the Tortoise and the Hare. While the hare confidently jumped here and there, following whatever struck his fancy, the tortoise stayed focused on the task at hand, pressing on toward the prize. Against all odds, the determined tortoise won the race, illustrating a valuable attribute of our own Christian walk: Slow and steady wins the race.

Read Hebrews 12:1-2 with 2 Timothy 4:7 before answering the following questions:

What steps must we take in order to "run the race successfully"?

How would you define endurance?

In what way did Jesus finish the race?

What does it mean to "keep the faith" and how are we to find the strength for the task?

Perseverance never asks us to come in first place, just to finish the race.

Perseverance has its price, but the reward always exceeds the cost. If you're getting slammed by Satan, then I congratulate you. That makes you a threat to him, which is the highest compliment you will ever get. It's inevitable that when the enemy strikes out at you in force, it is the spiritual repercussion of a job well done. That was never more evident than in the first few years of building the foundation of The Crossing.

It was in the first year after opening the doors of our new church that I was struck with Bell's palsy. For three months it left half of my face disfigured, drooping and numb. With my nose twisted, my lips slanted, cheek warped and distorted, it would have made it easy to hide in shame, choosing to give up the pulpit. Instead, I spoke boldly, saliva flying from my mouth. Neither vanity nor pride nor ego could silence me. And never did I hear a disparaging remark or see a judgmental glance. Only "Great message today, Pastor Paul!"

Through it all, I remained undaunted to preach what God had called me to. I refused to let the enemy derail my ministry and the work we were doing. For this, the church thrived and grew, even as I struggled with the condition. I never questioned God's sovereignty, but clung to Romans 8:28, letting perseverance finish its work. By the end of my recovery, our congregation was stronger than ever.

During the second year of The Crossing, Vicki and I were making home improvements—a yard upgrade with red mulch. As someone who has never experienced allergies in my life, it was a shock to wake up the next day, on Easter Sunday morning, to a case of acute hives. My lips had swelled and the skin over my entire body had exploded in welts. I was positively hideous to look at. Again, I persevered, giving a powerful message on Christ's resurrection, despite any psychological embarrassment or physical discomfort.

The following night, in the early morning hours, Vicki rushed me to the emergency room where they started an I.V. of medication to bring down the raging inflammation. A couple of hours later (with Vicki's nonstop prayer intercession), I was released to go home. Satan lost again.

> *You have heard of the perseverance of Job and seen the*
> *end intended by the Lord—that the Lord is very*
> *compassionate and merciful.*
>
> **JAMES 5:11**

In the fourth year at The Crossing, during a Jamestown, Tennessee camping excursion with our horses, we prepared to ride The Big Southfork with a group of friends. That morning we hit the trail to ride the ridges and wade through majestic streams and lush woods. At the end of the day, the horses, eager to be back at the hitching rail, picked up their pace and we let them run. When Vicki tried to rein in her mare, she was thrown to the ground between two giant boulders—a foot in either direction, her story would end here.

As she tried to stand up but couldn't, a sick feeling came over me as I realized she was seriously injured. With the sound of sirens approaching, all I could do was helplessly wait. At a small local hospital, the next few hours were a nightmare as I stayed by her side. In the morning, the doctor gave me a laundry list of sustained injuries: a broken pelvic bone and sacrum, which was causing internal bleeding, along with a punctured lung. Surprisingly, these injuries were secondary to the ten broken ribs, two of which were putting her aorta at high risk of laceration.

She may have survived the fall, but she could still die at any moment.

They quickly loaded us into an ambulance and sped down the highway, sirens blaring, toward the University of Tennessee. It was only then that I completely understood just how dangerous the situation was—life and death.

It's in moments like these that your prayers become very simple: "Please, Jesus, don't take her yet."

The coming days were an endless conversation with Jesus as the waiting continued. Incredibly, it was only nine days later that she was released from the hospital to recuperate at home. After three months, the orthopedic doctor declared her miraculously healed with no residual symptoms.

> *You must stay upon the Lord; and come what may—winds, waves… roaring breakers—no matter what, you must lash yourself to the helm, and hold fast your confidence in God's faithfulness…His everlasting love in Christ Jesus.*
>
> **RICHARD FULLER**

Let's read Romans 5:3-5. It tells us that suffering produces endurance in us.

Write down the two attributes that come through perseverance:

Why does hope never disappoint?

Why are we to glory in suffering?

When discouragement has threatened to overwhelm you, in what way(s) did God help you to persevere?

I will never leave you nor forsake you.
HEBREWS 13:5

PERSEVERANCE THROUGH PRAYER

Is there anything that defines our faith like that of persistent prayer? Week after week, sometimes year after year, we come, begging God for another's salvation, another healing, a personal request for relief. And even though there seems to be no change no matter how hard or diligently we pray, we stubbornly refuse to give up, believing God can and will answer us.

I wonder how many folks have died, praying for the salvation of a loved one, and later watched them burst through the gates of heaven with a hallelujah! Then there are people we love who have been diagnosed with a life-threatening disease, and though we don't worry about their salvation, we simply can't imagine the world without them in it. And so, we pray.

Kingston was six years old when he was diagnosed with leukemia. One night, I received a call and rushed to the hospital, convinced that I needed to prepare his mother, Jenni, for her impending loss—such was the progression of Kingston's disease. As I began speaking to her in a gentle yet sympathetic voice, she looked at me through those fiery blue eyes and stated, "My son will not die. God will heal him."

Today, Kingston is a healthy ten-year-old thanks to a mother's persevering prayer and a faith that moved a mountain. It was her proclamation of healing and continued faith that wouldn't let go. Like the man who fought with an angel all night to find his hip out of joint, but his prayer fully answered.

Only three years later, Jenni would find herself in a hospice facility due to cancer, surrounded by her husband and five children. She died Christmas Eve with a look of sweet recognition as she gazed up at someone or something we couldn't see. With her uncommon passion to meet

Jesus face-to-face, I believe she was hearing a "Hallelujah" as another saint prepared to pass through heaven's gates.

> *Their voice was heard; and their prayer came up to*
> *His holy dwelling place, to heaven.*
> **2 CHRONICLES 30:27**

> *There is great power to be had in persevering prayer.*
> **ANDREW MURRAY**

When the Roberts came to The Crossing, Emily was fifteen years old, non-verbal, and displayed something akin to extreme autism. Her mother, Amy, and her family had been called to a type of perseverance that few others experience.

When we realized what Amy was coping with, we immediately organized a rotation of volunteers to sit with Emily, keeping her settled in a quiet room watching television, while the rest of the family was able to enjoy the Sunday service.

What seemed like a small thing to us offered a much-needed respite to Amy, as she and her family were free to worship without the anxiety of Emily possibly disrupting others.

Over time as I got to know Amy, she began to open up about what life was like with Emily. I learned that it was a rare occasion when the family could go out together as Emily couldn't be left alone. Even getting gasoline for the car was filled with drama. Once, when Amy got out of her car to fill the tank, Emily became so upset, that it caused bystanders to become suspicious. From then on, Amy was forced to plan out even the smallest of errands. Just escaping to the front porch for a tranquil moment alone was impossible for Amy.

Only families of a disabled child can fully appreciate the sacrifices they make for an emotionally challenged child in the home. Many people would have placed her in an institution when she was little, but Amy insisted that Emily complete special needs school to equip her for as normal a life as possible.

In Luke 11:9-13, is there a progression of urgency in prayer?

Is there a difference between asking, seeking, and knocking?

Why do you believe God waits to answer prayer?

Week after week, Amy came to church with bruises and suffering back pain, but trusted God to give her the strength and courage to follow His lead. As Emily's graduation day approached, the church family began praying for Amy and Emily. Oh, how tender God is toward the persevering love of a mother.

Emily is now twenty-two and resides in the group home of Amy's choice. As any parent of a child with disabilities will tell you, Amy still has challenges with Emily. But she has seen firsthand God's faithfulness, and knows He has got her little girl in the palm of His hand.

As for Amy, or "Mamie," we see much more of her at church these days. She serves in the nursery and loves her "mini" fan club. What a gift it is for her to have the freedom to flourish in God's plan for her life. She is the true example of Romans chapter five: from tribulation to perseverance, from perseverance to character, from character to hope.

> *"A bend in the road is not the end of the road unless you fail to make the turn."*
> **HELEN KELLER**

> *"Perseverance is not a long race; it is many short races one after the other."*
>
> **WALTER ELLIOT**

I am a fortunate soul to have had a front row seat to the many stories of persevering prayer and the answers and divine assistance that came to meet them. It is no mystery that "longsuffering" is a fruit of the Spirit, for it is a blessing and not a curse. So be of good cheer, that your God considers you worthy to partake of its rich lessons.

Let's read 2 Corinthians 12:9-10 and answer the questions below:

How do we activate God's grace? What posture should we take?

_____

_____

_____

Is Paul talking about mental weakness, physical weakness, spiritual weakness? Explain.

_____

_____

_____

What is meant when Paul says he will "boast" in his weakness?

_____

_____

_____

What do we gain by embracing our own weaknesses?

The apostle Paul would face emotional discouragement, mental opposition, religious discrimination, and physical exhaustion throughout his ministry, but never spiritual doubt. The power of Christ took him from persecution to perseverance; from pursuing the called to answering the call. Paul fell head over heels in love with Jesus—no matter how difficult, dangerous, inconvenient, unpopular, or deadly it would be.

With every act of perseverance, Paul found strength in knowing he was one step closer to his goal. He was so persuaded that his fellow man needed to know Jesus Christ, that there was no price he was unwilling to pay to make that happen. Can you imagine the victory he achieved the day he died? He indeed won the marathon of all time.

What is your greatest goal in life? In what area, aspiration, or trial are you wanting the strength to persevere? Look to Jesus for His supernatural grace, and in His patience you will find perseverance.

And let us not grow weary while doing good,
for in due season we shall reap if we do not lose heart.
GALATIANS 6:9

Got It!

How has God enriched your understanding of perseverance through this stone?

It's time to *Dig Deeper!* Take a breath and think back on the ground we've covered, particularly in this stone. One might think that it is the least romantic of the stones, but I assure you that it is a gem of the rarest quality to the Lord. I hope the scriptures below will inspire you to a deeper understanding of the importance of perseverance.

"Watch, stand fast in the faith, be brave, be strong."
1 CORINTHIANS 16:13

"Therefore I ask that you do not lose heart at my tribulations for you, which is your glory."
EPHESIANS 3:13

"Bu as for you, brethren, do not grow weary in doing good."
2 THESSALONIANS 3:13

In the space below, record what new concepts you added to your foundation of perseverance by digging deeper:

_____

_____

STONE #10

Forgiveness

For if you forgive [people] their transgressions, your heavenly Father will also forgive you.

MATTHEW 6:14

I've heard of a ranch in a beautiful area along some foothills near a place called Compassion Valley. It was owned by a kind man with plenty of hired hands and a couple of sons who helped him with the cattle. The rancher loved his boys equally, and provided a good living for them. All seemed perfect until his youngest said he was leaving—no reason other than to get out and see what he was missing.

"Since I'm in your will and get half of your estate," he said, never pretending he would return or see his father alive again, "just give me my cut now." How heartbreaking those words must have been. But loving his child the way he did, the father divided his wealth, paid his son, and watched him walk away.

I suppose there are a lot of young men who feel dictated to by their dads, only to set out in search of greener pastures, just as this one did. And with plenty of cash in his pocket and a head full of dreams, he arrived in a foreign destination where exotic women and spirited nightlife gave him everything he bargained for. There he blew every penny, but his partying days were short-lived when the funds ran out along with his questionable company.

Broke and alone, he had few options and ended up working a dirty, manual labor job on a farm for room and board—a far cry from his comfortable ranch home and loving family.

When starvation set in, the young man asked his employer if he could trouble him for a meal, but he was flatly refused. Humiliated, he found himself brooding over the hog slop. "Even my dad's hired hands are fed like kings, and here I'm thinking about stealing the feed out of the pig's trough." So, with a tattered ego and in bare feet, he headed back to his native land.

I will arise and go to my father.
LUKE 15:18

While the son had been away, his dad had agonizingly watched for him every day, hoping and praying he would see his youngest again. But even through an empty horizon and the fear that his son had perished, he continued to pray and have faith. One day, he saw a speck in the distance, slowly growing bigger, closer. The father began to cry as his son came into view, haggard, thin, and threadbare. His dad bolted out to meet him, grabbed him by the scruff and hugged him with all his might, then kissed him.

Ashamed, his son said, "Dad, I've hurt you and God so badly, and I don't deserve your pity or your forgiveness or even to be your son anymore. Just hire me and I'll work for you. Please say you will."

But all his father could do was call out to his foreman, "Get a warm coat, my best, and some shoes for his feet! And prepare our biggest calf for slaughter and throw it on the BBQ! My son was dead, and is alive again!"

When the ranch owner's oldest son came in from the furthest field and saw that his little brother had returned—not reprimanded but celebrated—he was livid. He took his dad aside and yelled at him angrily, "All my life I've worked my hands raw for you. But when my brother quits, blows all your hard-earned money on girls, then comes back with nothing, you throw him a bash? I can't believe this!"

With compassion still shimmering in his eyes, his father answered, "I know that you're always here with me. Son, look around—all of this is yours. You've lost nothing. But your brother was hopelessly lost in every way but has come to his senses. It's right that we thank God for it."

Forgiveness unleashes joy. It brings peace. It washes the slate clean.
It sets all the highest values of love in motion.
GEORGE MACDONALD

In this story found in Luke 15:11-24, it tells of a young man who "had it all" but still wasn't satisfied. The modern-day version is all too familiar in our current society. Perhaps you know a prodigal son; a child who had good parents and a secure home, attended church every Sunday (perhaps more), but still walked away from God.

What do you suppose motivated the rancher's son to take the Wilderness Way?

What circumstances occurred that finally got his attention?

How did his attitude change, and what was the result?

How did his father respond when he returned home?

Did the son deserve the grace and mercy of his father?

What was the older brother's reaction to the father's lavish forgiveness, and what was the father's response to him?

Looking back over your own life, was there a time when you went the Wilderness Way? If so, what did God do to call you back to Himself?

That, my friends, is the prototype of our heavenly Father's forgiveness. Whether a prodigal child has been brought up with the love of God in their heart and home, or if it was absent and they were left to fend for themselves without the knowledge of Jesus's love and forgiveness, it's all the same. If one walks contrary to God's will, you are at the mercy of the darkness.

For those who have been blessed enough to enjoy a Christian household, and if they end up walking away, God will allow it for a time. But you can bet that He will always work to bring them back to the road that leads home—to sweet forgiveness and restoring fellowship with Him. Just as the father's joy overflowed as he ran to meet his son, so our God will run to you. If you're not right with God, why wait? Run back to Him in repentance, for Jesus delights in a repentant heart.

As far as the east is from the west, so far has [Jesus] removed our transgressions from us.

PSALM 103:12

The idea of forgiveness isn't hard to comprehend, but as most of us know, the act of forgiving can be much tougher, especially when we've been hurt. Our hearts get broken and suddenly, the pain inflicted upon us is too great to excuse. When someone close to us has betrayed us, the disloyalty can be impossible to pardon. So we end the relationship instead of pursuing reconciliation. Other times, we're the one doing the hurting, and lose a friend because they're unwilling to forgive.

Before I began building a foundation in Christ, I didn't even have the desire to forgive. I rather enjoyed my grudges. Treating them like a pet, I would hold them close to me, pet them and nurture them, taking pride in "being right" and defending my position to anyone who questioned it.

Truthfully, self-righteous anger has power, but not of God. Until we reconcile our past with God and others, our future will be affected, perhaps more than we dare realize.

However, the more we seek God, the more realistic our view of self and our responsibility to own our imperfections become. No human being is perfect; no one never makes a mistake; no one is celebrated all the time. There will be crossroads in every life where a choice to forgive and/or long for forgiveness must be made. My friend, make the right choice.

Bitterness, unforgiveness, and holding a grudge are like drinking poison and waiting for the other person to suffer.

AMAZING GRACE

The hymn Amazing Grace was written in 1772 by John Newton, a ship captain and slave trader who took an active part in the dehumanization of God's creatures. His awe-inspiring transformation from reviled profiteer to beloved Anglican minister and respected abolitionist still resonates with us today. So when he wrote the words "that saved a wretch like me," he knew God's forgiveness better than most. In the latter part of his life, the lyrics "was blind, but now I see" had come true as he lost his sight completely. I like to think that's when John finally saw God in absolute clarity.

> *The unchangeableness of the Lord's love, and the riches*
> *of His mercy, are likewise more illustrated by the multiplied pardons*
> *He bestows upon His people — than if they*
> *needed no forgiveness at all.*
> **JOHN NEWTON**

With spiritual maturity comes sensitivity to the Holy Spirit, which involves us with Him on a deeply personal level. Nothing is worth the cost of grieving His sweet Spirit. Who enjoys hurting someone they love? There is also power in refusing to allow pride to dominate a heart that belongs to Jesus. Without the stone of forgiveness, it would be impossible to have a foundation in Christ. And nothing displays Christ's power and love like the heart that learns the freedom in releasing a grudge.

Let's read Genesis 2:16-17, and then skim chapter 3 to get a perspective on the following exercise:

Explain in your own words what took place.

Would you say that Adam and Eve willfully sinned?

Forgiveness

What were the consequences of their sin?

_____
_____
_____

What evidence shows that God forgave Adam and Eve?

_____
_____
_____
_____

Did they deserve God's forgiveness?

_____
_____
_____
_____

After everything God had done for His beloved children, can you imagine the heartache he experienced with their disappointing behavior? Did you catch how Adam even tried suggesting that the mess they created was somehow God's fault—"the woman You put here with me." But it was Eve who correctly identified her enemy, the enemy of mankind ever since.

> *He who covers a transgression seeks love,*
> *But he who repeats a matter separates friends.*
> **PROVERBS 17:9**

Before that fateful day, there was no need for God's forgiveness. He had given Adam and Eve the perfect life, lacking nothing. Still, they managed to destroy everything due to one wrong choice, then another and another. This world has been infected by sin ever since, just as it has been passed on from generation to generation. We all sin because of poor choices, pride, and fear. Yet God's forgiveness remains.

Thousands of years later, another tree would spring up, marked for a radical purpose.

The "tree" that Christ would hang upon to dissolve our transgressions, to forgive sin completely, and to reconcile us to Him forever, was a tree planted for the unbelievable sacrifice—a kind of forgiveness this world has never known before.

Read Romans 5:8 and complete this verse:

"But God demonstrates His own love toward us…"

What does Ephesians 4:32 instruct us to do?

Why is it so important for us to treat each other this way?

Outside of God's amazing grace, our bad choices would still be our downfall, just as it was for our forefathers. Today, we continue to hurt God (and each other) in spite of our love for Him. God's spotless lamb, slain for us—though we remain sinners, sometimes willfully—is continuously there forgiving us. It's a full-time job. What can we possibly do to deserve such extravagant love?

The sad fact is, we have a sin problem! If we could not only share enough empathy to practice forgiveness, instead of clinging to our pride, what a wonderful world it would be.

> *He has not dealt with us according to our sins, nor punished us according to our iniquities. For as the heavens are high above the earth,*
> *so great is His mercy toward those who fear Him.*
> **PSALM 103:10-11**

When I read Colossians 3:12-15, it puts it all in perspective. If ever there was a question about how Christians are to treat one another, it is stated without reservation in this scripture. I'd like you to commit it to memory, and also answer the questions below:

As God's elect, what are we to "put on"?

_____

_____

_____

What is it that we must do when dealing with each other?

_____

_____

_____

Which is the most important thing to practice (verse 14) that will enable us to forgive?

_____

_____

_____

What is the element that connects all virtues, and what is the outcome?

When working on a home improvement project, have you ever forgotten to add the bonding agent to a product? You'll know if you have, because the result is a mess! And like that bonding agent that adheres to the most unlikely of surfaces, love is God's bonding agent that brings us together beyond any severing. God is love, therefore if we live in Him, how can we possibly think we can walk with the bitterness of unforgiveness abiding in us?

Who is it time for you to forgive?

Like any project with a "to do" list, I'm going to challenge you right now to write down who it is that you need to forgive. Think back through the past weeks, months, even years, and record the names of the people and the transgression(s) that have kept you from moving forward in God's love and mercy.

Bravo! I knew you could do it. And if you should, at times, forget this charitable step in your faith walk, remember this scripture:

> *[Love] is not provoked, thinks no evil; does not*
> *rejoice in iniquity, but rejoices in the truth.*
> **1 CORINTHIANS 13:5-6**

It is written in Ephesians 4:26, "do not let the sun go down on your wrath," and this was my heart-cry as several times, others had wronged me, or I had wronged another. The Bible instructs us to go to our brother who sins against us. By doing so, we thwart Satan's efforts to plant seeds of hurt and bitterness.

Sadly, we can't expect this will always resolve our differences. No, for a God-glorifying result, it takes two softened hearts to yield to one another in the Lord—a rare thing. However, if I go with a humble spirit of reconciliation instead of a determination to prove that I'm right, my heart can walk away in peace, leaving it to the Lord to sort things out.

FORGIVING YOURSELF

While it's all well and good to find it in your heart to forgive someone you feel has wronged you, to forgive yourself for something is quite another. We hurt others, and with the aid of a healthy conscience, we feel bad. We may muster up the humility to go to the person and ask for forgiveness, and they accept. Why then, do we leave carrying a burden we thought we got rid of?

Then there are folks who have had truly heinous things done to them—spousal abuse, parental neglect, verbal cruelty, and physical assault—and were still able to forgive their perpetrator. Yet they remained damaged due to the shame they felt, as if they were responsible for the mistreatment. Are you one of them? Is it time you forgave yourself for something that was out of your control?

Do you believe what God says about Himself? Then dare to believe you are who God says you are!

Let's read Galatians 4:7 and absorb its meaning before you go on to answer the following questions:

Who does God say you are?

_____

_____

_____

Now read 1 Corinthians 6:11 before answering the question below:

Who does God say you are?

_____

_____

Read 2 Corinthians 5:17 and answer this question:

Who does God say you are?

_____

_____

Believe it or not, failure to forgive yourself will be a weight from the past that you drag along with you until it exhausts you. It can keep you repeating old habits that Satan can and will use to defeat you.

Imagine if you had a child who came to you, admitted wrongdoing, and asked for forgiveness. What a joyful exchange and delight as you completely forgave them. Now imagine that same child coming to you, begging for forgiveness morning after morning, even though you forgave them again and again. But they fail to realize that you are no longer concerned with their past mistakes.

Have you struggled to give the same grace to yourself that God has freely given you?

> *Behold what manner of love the Father has bestowed on us,*
> *that we should be called children of God! Therefore the world*
> *does not know us, because it did not know Him.*
>
> **1 JOHN 3:1**

Even a negative focus on self is a focus on self.

Even a negative focus on self is still a focus on self. Becoming part of the body of Christ puts us in a relationship with one another, which comes with responsibilities. That means we hold the power to break or to bless—ourselves or those who share our faith.

Forgiveness is not simply a means to ease the pain of the past. It is an attribute of the Holy Spirit given to free our spirit from the sting of betrayal, sorrow, and bitterness.

What does Romans 12:19 tell us *not* to do?

_____

_____

_____

What does it tell us that we *should* do?

_____

_____

_____

Write down what God says *He* will do:

_____

_____

_____

A recent story emerged from Texas about an 18-year-old boy and a woman accused of shooting his brother. As the boy took the witness stand, he looked directly at the accused and said, "I love you like anyone else. I want the best for you, and I think my brother would want you to give your life to Christ."

He then asked the judge if he could give the woman a hug—a request the judge granted. He stepped off the witness stand and met her in front of the judge's bench. As they embraced, he whispered private words as she broke into sobs.

Moments later, the judge spoke to the accused privately, hugged her, and appeared to give her words of hope. Then, amazingly, the judge handed her a Bible! What beautiful, Christlike actions in a world filled with hatred and division.

Though the boy could have easily justified any bitterness, he chose to elude the trap of unforgiveness that could have ensnared him for a lifetime. It reflects the perfect image of Christ in the midst of a sad and horrific story, magnifying the power of forgiveness.

> *And whatever you do in word or deed, do all in the name of the Lord Jesus, giving thanks to God the Father through Him.*
> **COLOSSIANS 3:17**

Read Mark 11:25 and write down what you can expect to receive when you sow forgiveness.

"Whatever a man sows, so he shall reap" is God's natural law. We all need forgiveness. We all need grace. We all need love. When we choose forgiveness, a strong, peaceful, and unshakable stone becomes embedded into our foundation.

> *Do not be deceived, God is not mocked; for whatever a man sows, that he will also reap.*
> **GALATIANS 6:7**

Got It!

How has God enriched your understanding of forgiveness through this stone?

_____
_____
_____
_____

It's time to *Dig Deeper!* From the prodigal son, to Adam and Eve, to Calvary's cross, it is all within our reach if we will only seek forgiveness and to forgive. I hope that the scriptures below will strengthen your will to do as the Father commands, and in doing so, you will reap a harvest of healing.

*"Judge not, and you shall not be judged.
Condemn not, and you shall not be condemned.
Forgive, and you will be forgiven."*

LUKE 6:37

"There will be more joy in heaven over one sinner who repents than over ninety-nine just persons who need no repentance."

LUKE 15:7

"He who covers his sins will not prosper, but whoever confesses and forsakes them will have mercy."

PROVERBS 28:13

In the space below, record what new concepts you added to your foundation of forgiveness by digging deeper:

STONE #11

Repentance

For I acknowledge my transgressions, and my sin is always before me.

PSALM 51:3

Repentance. It is a word loaded with Christian significance. It brings an emotional reaction to most of us—hopefully—and we immediately feel our human nature and spiritual obedience being tested. For followers of Christ, it reaches far deeper than what the world can (or will) grasp. We owe our very faith to the word, for without it, we are denying God's plan of reconciliation established through His Son.

But for argument's sake, let's first look at the description of repentance in the Oxford Dictionary. Its definition reads, "The acknowledgment and condemnation of one's sins, coupled with a turning to God. It includes sorrow for the sin committed, confession of guilt, and the purpose of amendment." That's a very good start, but for believers, the word is more than an intellectual explanation or a passing thought when we are dealing with guilt. It is a way of life.

In the Book of Acts written by the Apostle Luke, he tells us to, "Repent therefore and be converted, that your sins may be blotted out, so that times of refreshing may come from the presence of the Lord" (3:19). Repentance isn't just a good idea, but a necessity in a blueprint for our conversion. Without it, there is no transformation.

I'd like for us to think about five levels of repentance that, like the foundational stones all working together to build a wall of unshakable faith, will help you understand its importance.

1. Repentance is accepting Christ: It is a non-negotiable term acknowledging our imperfectness.

2. Repentance is ongoing conviction: It is the Holy Spirit keeping us right with God.

3. Repentance is being obedient: It is following God's command to change.

4. Repentance is worship: It tears down self to lift up the Lord.

5. Repentance is the model of Christianity: It sets the example of humility for others to follow.

While in one sense, repentance opens the initial door to salvation, over time, our need for repentance only grows as our faith grows. In my experience, the more I developed and matured as a Christian, it seemed the more I was aware of the Holy Spirit's conviction. And with knowledge comes wisdom. I finally realized that repentance was an ongoing part of my walk with Jesus.

My friend, there is no shame in recognizing our need for continuous cleansing of mind, body, and soul.

> *Repentance is the sweet fruit that comes from faith in the Savior*
> *and involves turning toward God and away from sin.*
> **DAVID A BEDNAR**

THE POWER TO CHANGE

Beyond the verbal acknowledgment of wrongs, repentance goes a step further. It is the act of leaving what God has prohibited and returning to what He has commanded. In other words, it isn't enough to feel badly about offending God. It takes more than our apology, but we must leave behind the offensive behavior to embrace our calling of transparency and grace. This includes genuine remorse for what we've done, and our intention to not do it again.

Now, I know what you're thinking... *there are some things I just keep doing, no matter how many times I've promised God and myself that I wouldn't.* To that, I quote the Apostle Paul from Romans 7:15, 24: "For what I am doing, I do not understand. For what I will to do, that I do not practice; but what I hate, that I do... O wretched man that I am! Who will deliver me from this body of death?" Does that sum it up for you?

That is exactly why repentance is so important. No matter how disciplined we are, no matter what lengths we take to avoid sin, we end up sinning anyway. So why do we keep trying to live a perfect life? Because God has called us to change—not in our power, but in His.

> *I, therefore, the prisoner of the Lord, beseech you to walk worthy of the calling with which you were called.*
> **EPHESIANS 4:1**

It's seeing ourselves differently—the old self and who we were, in contrast to the "new man" and who we are now. It's a "do-over"; a second chance, an opportunity to start again and be someone completely different. That is an extraordinary gift we've been given.

Let's read Ephesians 4:17-24 before answering the questions below:

What is the contrast between the old man and the new?

_____
_____
_____

What does it mean to "be renewed" in the attitude of our mind?

_____
_____
_____

What does it say we were created to be like?

_____
_____
_____

True repentance will always draw us away from an offensive past lifestyle into a righteous lifestyle. Just as new wine cannot be poured into an old wineskin, as it will only break apart the old and ruin the new (Mark 2:23), so we are to leave behind our old way of living to pursue a rejuvenated life in Christ.

Let's read 2 Timothy 2:19-23 and let it sink in before answering the following questions:

What is it that Christians are to depart from?

How do we become vessels of honor for the Master?

Moving on to 2 Timothy 2:24-26, what is the job of being a servant of the Lord?

What stone have we already covered that results in repentance?

He who covers his sins will not prosper, but whoever confesses and forsakes them will have mercy.
PROVERBS 28:13

WHEN IT COMES TO OTHERS

Just as we come to God to repent of our sins toward Him, it is equally important for us to approach others and ask their forgiveness for wrongs we've committed against them. Why does that seem so dangerous? What is it that we risk by saying we're sorry to someone who deserves an apology? They will either receive it in kindness and appreciation and forgive, or they will hold onto their anger, doubt our authenticity, and reject us. Both require our sincerity, and both should clear us of any guilt.

How our repentance is received is not up to us.

Repentance knocks down the wall of unforgiveness. Whether telling someone how sorry you are or teaching the power of forgiveness, how our repentance is received is not up to us.

Now let's examine Mark 6:7-13 and answer these questions:

What power did Jesus give to the disciples?

_____

_____

_____

What message did they preach?

_____

_____

_____

What did "shaking off the dust under their feet" symbolize?

_____

_____

_____

Repent, and be free my friend.

Another definition that I think fits the stone of repentance is *communion*: "The sharing or exchanging of intimate thoughts and feelings, especially when the exchange is on a mental or spiritual level."[3]

Isn't that a beautiful description of God's invitation to enjoy intimate fellowship with Him? But communion is more than that. It should be a time of remembrance, confession, cleansing, and encouragement as we rejoice in the provisional power of God.

As we partake in this very personal exchange, we are to examine ourselves for any "wicked way" in us (Psalm 139:23-24) that could keep us from moving forward without guilt or condemnation. It is a time to repent and be refreshed in the Lord.

> *But let a man examine himself, and so let him eat of the bread and drink of the cup. For he who eats and drinks in an unworthy manner eats and drinks judgment to himself, not discerning the Lord's body.*
> **1 CORINTHIANS 11:28-29**

As I grew up in a Baptist church, communion would be served about once per quarter, with the elements passed up and down the aisle toward the end of service. However, I don't recall anyone making their way to the altar as part of taking communion. The altar seemed reserved for those coming forward for salvation at the pastor's invitation.

As I prayed over The Crossing in preparation for the opening, the Lord impressed upon me to offer communion every Sunday, a new concept for me. We would invite believers to get up from their seats and come forward to share in communion. Like worshipping and praying, communion (which includes repentance) is a practice of obedience that we share with others — side by side.

I was amazed when, upon opening Sunday, and every Sunday since, I have witnessed the altar filled with people doing business with God. Some bring the elements to the altar and consume them after prayer. Others pray and then rise to make their way to the table. Much mentioned in the Bible, the altar has always been a powerful place to come before the Lord. At the altar, we

---

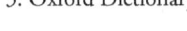

3. Oxford Dictionary

Repentance  203

learn humility, accountability, and how to encourage and pray for and with one another. This excludes any judgment calls we may harbor in our thoughts about the challenges faced by other folks.

In Romans 2:1-4, Paul draws a parallel between our repentance and our judgment of others.

Why is it unwise for us to judge others—what can we expect from God when we do?

What is the danger of refusing to give grace to others?

What are the riches of God that Paul talks about, and what do they lead to? List them.

How often do you find yourself repenting? You can better believe the Apostle Paul kept short accounts with God. As a result, he wrote some of the most relational scripture in the Bible.

If you have ever been drawn to repentance by the goodness and patience of God, if you have learned the freedom and blessings of repentance in undeserved forgiveness, shouldn't the natural progression be a soft, repentant attitude toward others? Yet, too often, when we feel that twinge of conviction about something we have said or done against another, we lack the courage or humility to make amends.

When we lose our judgmental attitude toward people, that is when we will most likely have less to apologize for. Knowing how hard it is to face someone and say, "I didn't mean it. I'm so sorry," should hone our empathy to be sweeter and to overlook an offense, just as God's Word exhorts us to do.

I've seen the hardest of hearts melt at a genuine "I'm sorry." And aren't we quicker to throw away our anger toward someone when they come to us in meekness and honest regret? Therefore, shouldn't we react the same when we are confronted by someone about our own sin?

Read 2 Samuel 12:1-14 and ponder its meaning before answering the questions below:

What was King David's initial attitude when the prophet Nathan confronted him?

_____
_____
_____

How did King David finally respond—what did he say?

_____
_____
_____

What happened after David repented?

_____
_____
_____

In His goodness and mercy, God will often send someone to confront us with our sin. Do not despise the discipline of God. David went on to write most of the Book of Psalms in which he poured out his wisdom regarding repentance. He had come to understand that sin against another person is sin against God. Repentance fills the chasm between our selfish faults and God's atoning grace.

Who can understand his errors? Cleanse me from secret faults.
Keep back Your servant also from presumptuous sins;
let them not have dominion over me. Then I shall be blameless, and I shall be
innocent of great transgression.

PSALM 19:12-13

Be gentle toward the godly person who cares enough to confront you about your sin. I can tell you from my own dealings that it is not an easy thing to do, even when covered by prayer. And if they got it all wrong? It happens. Just bathe it in grace and move on in the Lord.

Let Philippians 4:4-7 rule over you: Be united. Be joyful. Be prayerful.

I repented of my sin and gave my heart to Jesus when I was twelve, at least as much as any

12-year-old can. It's true, at that age I didn't have much to walk away from, but I consciously began my journey with Christ. I started paying more attention in church, and even took my Bible to school. That is until I grew older, and the temptations of this world began to lure me away from the God I loved.

Satan had been watching and knew a youngster wasn't much of a threat, but as a young man on fire for Jesus, that was another story. And just as he's known to do, the devil began to dangle the kind of shiny bait a young man can seldom resist—fast cars, girls, and power. I use that last word in relation to becoming the youngest manager Steak 'n Shake ever had.

Before long, ego took over, and I no longer had time for church. Jesus became increasingly absent from my life to the point He had disappeared altogether. Of course that's not true, but when you're chasing your own desires, it's hard to see Him. Looking back now, like Job, God had allowed Satan to tempt me. Still, as Jesus was ever present—never leaving me as He promised—Satan was only allowed to go so far.

Still, off I went on The Wilderness Way.

Repentance can lose its charm if the heart fails to seek a solid foundation in Christ.

Over the years, Satan would continue trying to destroy my integrity, my family, and every value I held dear. He nearly succeeded. *"Nevertheless, God…"*

> *Nevertheless [God] regarded their affliction,*
> *when He heard their cry;*
> *and for their sake He remembered His covenant,*
> *and relented according to the*
> *multitude of His mercies.*
>
> **PSALM 106:44**

Needless to say, by the time I had come to the end of myself—a far cry from a 12-year-old's innocent confessions—I had finally learned the valuable life lessons in God's school of hard knocks. I was ready to surrender my will to Him, and as you can imagine, I had some serious repenting to do.

It's interesting to consider that in God's eyes, repentance is repentance, whether offered up by a little boy with a scraped knee or a grown man with a battered conscience. Both hold the power of salvation that preserves and protects life—the life He foresees in the future, say a man who would one day become a preacher. I wouldn't recommend that fool's journey to anyone. Because of those long detours, I can only assume that I missed out on much of what God had originally planned for me and my family. But I suppose I was just that stubborn, and God took that into account.

The power and grace that repentance brings are wholly radical and undeserved, and I love Him all the more for it.

Let's read Psalm 32:3-5 together, and consider the questions below:

What was the result of David initially staying silent?

What was required of David to restore fellowship with God?

In the Book of Lamentations, read 3:40-44 and move on to the questions below:

When dealing with our transgressions, what does God instruct us to do and why?

What actions did God take that brought about their desire to repent?

How have you experienced God's call to repentance, and how did you respond?

Repentance is an ongoing, ever-deepening occurrence in a Christian's heart.

Have you ever (consciously or subconsciously) drifted apart from God to suddenly awaken one morning, realizing you were just going through the motions, and not knowing how you got so far away? When we are ready to face that kind of lethargic faith, sin is always the culprit. It distances us from the One who would have us "leap for joy" (Luke 6:23), but wind up feeling cut off from His very presence.

It is on the day we humble ourselves before the Lord, that we may again enjoy sweet fellowship with Him. I've preached over and over that God will not compromise with us. His statutes are set in stone—foundational stones for the building of His temple, which is us!

I encourage you to repent of gossip and words spoken harshly. Repent of wrong thoughts, pride, wasted time, irresponsible money management, and lost opportunities to speak life to those around you. If you can't find a reason to repent, repent for not seeing the need to repent! Repent or run the risk of finding yourself like the Pharisee in Luke 18:9-14. I urge you to read it and learn.

> *The Pharisee stood and prayed thus with himself,*
> *"God, I thank you that I am not like other men…"*
>
> **LUKE 18:11**

> *For everyone who exalts himself will be humbled,*
> *And he who humbles himself will be exalted.*
>
> **LUKE 18:14**

True repentance is not merely fixing something. It's becoming something.

Got It!

How has God enriched your understanding of repentance through this stone?

It's time to *Dig Deeper!* Repentance could well be the most uncomfortable stone to lift and carry. But once we have steadfastly placed it within our foundation of faith, oh, what strength and resilience our house will have against the enemy's wind, rain, and flood. We will remain unmoved in the power of humility and transparency.

> *"Do you despise the riches of His goodness, forbearance, and longsuffering, not knowing that the goodness of God leads you to repentance?"*
>
> **ROMANS 2:4**

> *"Therefore bear fruits worthy of repentance, and do not think to say to yourselves, 'We have Abraham as our father.' For I say to you that God is able to raise up children to Abraham from these stones."*
>
> **MATTHEW 3:8-9**

> *"Now I rejoice, not that you were made sorry, but that your sorrow led to repentance. For you were made sorry in a godly manner, that you might suffer loss from us in nothing."*
>
> **2 CORINTHIANS 7:9**

In the space below, record what new concepts you added to your foundation of repentance by digging deeper:

STONE #12

Security

What then shall we say to these things?
If God is for us, who can be against us?

ROMANS 8:31

There isn't a thing in this world that can promise us absolute security—not one. Government can't offer it, money can't secure it, and spouses can't guarantee it. As it is said, "Death and taxes are the only things guaranteed."

In comparison, what a gift the Lord has given us in this final foundational stone we will study. Through Jesus Christ, there is absolute, irrevocable security that no power on this earth can take away. The stronger our foundation in the previous stones discussed, the more fully we will appreciate the peace and security of knowing exactly who we are in Christ.

Truth and security are the bookends that hold all the foundation stones together—that is, unshakable security in our faith. And as Jesus Christ is the same yesterday, today, and forever (Hebrews 13:8), He is all the security we will ever need in this world, and in the next.

Jesus is all the security we will ever need in this world, and in the next.

Let's recap the Twelve Stones and how they build our security:

- **Truth:** We are secure in knowing God's Word is absolute truth. (John 18:37)

- **Obedience:** We are secure in knowing that obedience = blessings. (Deuteronomy 28:1-2)

- **Glory:** We are secure in knowing that we were created to bring God glory. (Romans 11:36)

- **Love:** We are secure in knowing God loves us, no matter what. (Luke 10:27)

- **Wisdom:** We are secure in knowing that Jesus gives us wisdom. (Proverbs 4:5-7)

- **Discernment:** We are secure in knowing discernment is ours through the Holy Spirit. (Philippians 1:9-10)

- **Humility:** We are secure in knowing that humility is strength, not weakness. (James 4:10)

- **Self-control:** We are secure in knowing that God control is self-control. (1 Corinthians 10:13)

- **Perseverance:** We are secure in knowing that slow and steady wins the race. (Hebrews 12:1)

- **Forgiveness:** We are secure in knowing that forgiveness is sweet. (Matthew 6:14)

- **Repentance:** We are secure in knowing that repentance brings forgiveness. (1 John 1:9)

- **Security:** We are secure in God's promises because He never changes. (Hebrews 13:8)

Security is the sum of all stones with its great value only realized when we release all dependence on the security of this world to lean totally on Christ.

And I give them eternal life, and they shall never perish;
neither shall anyone snatch them out of My hand.
JOHN 10:28

What could hold more value in life than knowing that nothing can ever snatch us from the hands of our loving Father? How could a child live in the light of their parents' love if they worried they were one mistake away from being lost or cast aside?

Knowing who we are in Christ gives us the security to live out and boldly speak His truths.

*One of the special marks of the Holy Ghost in the
Apostolic Church was the spirit of boldness.*

A.B. SIMPSON

I had owned Taylor Door for over thirty years when God called me to establish The Crossing. My business was the livelihood for my family and enabled me to decline a church salary for the first five years, desiring that the church establish a firm foundation before it began paying a pastor. However, the time and energy required to build a new church quickly took its toll.

For me to give the church my best, my son Ryan Dean, who was an employee at the time, was forced to take on more and more of the company duties. When that happened, I began to realize a change was coming. While Ryan fully supported my ministry and never complained, soon I began praying about how I might compensate him for his efforts.

When I realized God was calling me to trust Him further by giving over to my son half of what I had built, controlled, and reaped the benefits from over the years, questions about the unknown swirled in my mind. Would it interfere with our relationship? Would we see eye to eye? Would the company generate enough revenue to support the decision?

So many times from the pulpit I had challenged my congregation to step out in faith to see what God could do. And those impassioned speeches were always due to my own life experiences that proved the truth about God's promises.

As it turned out, my son and I have been in partnership now for eight years, and our relationship has only grown. The company is stronger than ever, blessing not one but two families. Ryan Dean continues to support me, not just in ministry, but as Vicki and I age. All that worry for nothing. There is simply no security this world has to offer that compares to knowing Jesus is holding you in His mighty grasp! Jesus Christ is all the security we will ever need.

*I will both lie down in peace, and sleep; for You alone,
O Lord, make me dwell in safety.*

PSALM 4:8

KNOW IT

I'm a "prop" preacher! From one Sunday to the next, my congregation never knows what they will find on stage. So when I began to teach The Wilderness Way series, a small cement mixer sat in plain view, as a new stone—from Truth to Security—appeared next to me each week.

For a sermon on eternal security, I laid the "Book of Life" open on an easel with names written in it. However, the book soon became a mess, as names were scratched out, added back, scratched out again, and new ones inserted. It was a creative depiction on how God's book of life would look if I based salvation on my feelings. The painful fact is, if we center salvation—for ourselves and for others—on our emotions, there would be no book at all.

The Book of 1 John, considered to be written by the Apostle John, tells us of our security in a way that is so relatable, I will repeat it here: "These things I have written to you who believe in the name of the Son of God, that you may know that you have eternal life, and that you may continue to believe in the name of the Son of God" (1 John 5:13). We can consider that a promise.

What does 1 John 5:13 tell us the basis for salvation is?

Backing up to the preceding verses, according to 1 John 5:1-5, what is the evidence of our "belief?"

In Romans 8:12-17, what further evidence is presented regarding our security in Christ?

Paul's dramatic statements to the new church in Rome offer us the same conviction. Do you live by the Spirit, putting the deeds of the flesh to death? Does the Spirit of God lead you? When you cry "Daddy!" does your spirit bear witness with His Spirit that you are His child? When trials come, do you know where to run?

There is not a point of doctrine that we should take more seriously than our salvation. Absolutely nothing can bring more power and peace to the Christian faith than that of our eternal security.

When we consider the magnitude of what Jesus did for us—to stand in proxy between God and our sins—there may come moments of doubt leading some of us to ask, "Am I saved?" If or when those thoughts arise, hit your knees and go to battle. You will rise a conqueror, confirmed by the Spirit. If you still aren't sure, then I hope you will read the final chapter of this book titled Salvation.

According to Romans 8:35-39, what can separate God's elect from His love?

Yet in all these things we are more than conquerors through Him who loved us.
ROMANS 8:37

For the mountains shall depart and the hills be removed,
but My kindness shall not depart from you.
Nor shall my covenant of peace be removed,
says the Lord, who has mercy on you.

ISAIAH 54:10

LIVE IT

As I mentioned in the introduction, God intended His people's exodus from Egypt to be a two-year journey into the Promised Land. However, due to the stubbornness and rebellion of their hearts, it turned into forty years of wandering the wilderness. Their refusal to trust God to go into the place of milk and honey reads like a Greek tragedy in Numbers 13-14. God had brought them out of slavery to absolute freedom and security, and this was their response:

"Why has the Lord brought us to this land to fall by the sword, that our wives and children should become victims? Would it not be better for us to return to Egypt?" (Numbers 14:3).

How quickly humans forget. Our attention span would be comical if it weren't for the damage it inflicts on our lives. God is still calling His people to go where He leads. Even though it may be challenging or frightening. I urge you to be careful to hear His voice, trusting He has His very best for you.

Though we may struggle to remember a lot of important promises, there is one fact that should never escape us: Even as God's people rebelled, refused to trust Him, accused Him of intending them harm, and desired to return to slavery, God never changed His mind about them. Just as He promised to take His people into the Promised Land, His promise of heaven is secure for us today.

Let's read Joshua 3:14-17 and answer the following questions:

What do you believe the significance is of crossing the Jordan on dry ground?

What did the priests have to do in order for the flood to recede?

Can you think of a deeper meaning the flood waters symbolize?

Now let's look at Joshua 4:1-3; 21-24, and think about the questions below:

Why did God command the Israelites to set up twelve stones?

Describe what the twelve stones (words) in this study mean to you:

How would you describe them to others?

The Crossing Church received its name based on the verses from Joshua. While crossing the Red Sea for us represents salvation, after a time of learning to love and trust God, we are required to step into the flood of life to cross over into a land where God's abundance awaits. For too many years, the Israelites refused to trust God, choosing to stay put, even though He had so much more for them — just on the other side of the river.

Can you imagine the people's hearts as they finally stood on the other side, laying the stones?

It's fascinating to think that those twelve stones still exist somewhere in the area of Gilgal, near Jericho, in the West Bank, buried beneath centuries of earth. So often, when life gets hard and we feel buried under a mountain of trouble, we forget what God has done for us — the absolute miracle of our salvation and the countless ways He has interceded throughout our lives.

Just as the stones were a memorial of remembrance for the Israelites, it is good for us to lay down markers to remember the Lord. Have you ever made a public profession of faith? Lay down that marker! Have you been baptized? Do you keep a journal of God's faithfulness? These can all be markers of remembrance. It's very special to look back through a journey fraught with raging currents of opposition to see how God lovingly carried you through them to dry land.

Don't ever forget what Jesus has done for you, on earth and in heaven!

I hope you don't misunderstand me; an abundant life is not the absence of trials. Battles were waiting on the other side of the Jordan for Israel, just as you and I face them today. But God is on both sides, then and now, always at work.

How does remembering what God has done for you help you stay faithful in the wilderness?

Read 1 Peter 2:9-10 and answer the questions below:

What does God call His people in these verses?

Who does the scripture say you were before you surrendered to Jesus?

What is your purpose on this earth?

Now let's read Psalm 91:14-16 and answer the next questions:

According to these verses, what exclusive promises do you find for those who love God?

What does it say we need to do first to receive such protection?

Johnny B! Where on earth does one begin in telling the story of John? Vicki and I first met Johnny when he was about twelve years old, as he grew up with our children in the same neighborhood. One summer, he came home from college declaring he had been "saved." Over the next twenty years, we've watched John simultaneously walk with God and the world, determinedly striving to build earthly security in his own power.

As the years rolled on, he married and had four beautiful daughters. The family would travel from Florida every year to visit us in Indiana, and we modeled the Christian life with Jesus as best we could. At times, I questioned Johnny's salvation, but there was something there. He had a genuine hunger for God, but also an intense attachment to the world. And in typical Johnny fashion, he would start a company, build it up, then just when he thought it was viable, the whole thing would fall apart. It was a disheartening pattern.

He eventually moved to Las Vegas where he partnered with ruthless men who almost had him imprisoned in an effort to steal his company shares. Due to this yo-yo life cycle, Johnny has slept in lavish suites at the Hilton and on derelict park benches as the battle for a calm "in between" raged on. He reminded me of Jacob, who fought with God but refused to let go of Him. Time and again, Johnny limped away; got up and fell again and again, until he finally let go and let Jesus have His way.

Today, John's business thrives as only God can prosper someone. Now he uses money—like a tool in God's shed—to enjoy his life, bless others, and facilitate God's work. Through all the ups and downs and God's dealings with him, Johnny has come to find his security in Christ alone.

God will greatly bless the man who has come to depend wholly on Him.

It was Johnny, in the spring of 2019, who blessed *us* with that all-expenses paid trip to Israel in appreciation for the many years we contended for his faith. If you asked today, he would tell you that the greatest gift in letting go and trusting Christ is that no matter what your condition—whether rich or poor—Jesus has you securely covered.

*Not that I speak in regard to need,
for I have learned in whatever state I am, to be content.*

PHILIPPIANS 4:11

God will greatly bless the man who has come to depend wholly on Him

This poem has resonated with many folks I've taught The Wilderness Way to over the years. I hope it encourages you as well to "get out of the boat" to live in the power, joy, and security of Jesus Christ.

The Rare Soldier

Merrily, merrily bobbing afloat,
Sits an army of Christians safe in the boat.

Servants aplenty, they go 'bout their jobs,
But seldom is seen the power of God.

Once in a while they sit up and take note,
As they watch the rare soldier climb out of the boat.

The ordinary man does extraordinary things,
As small steps of faith seem to take wings.

His joyful life, the rest wistfully see,
Safe in the boat, they sigh: I wish it were me.

Then all of a sudden, the soldier seems to fall,
And the rest wisely whisper, "We were right after all."

In comfortable boats, filled with safe ministry,
They never heard Jesus ask, "Will you come out to me?"

Crossing life's ocean, they'll make it to shore,
But find when they get there, Jesus had so much more.

VICKI TAYLOR

It was an experience to walk the streets of old Jerusalem amongst God's chosen people. Nothing models God's love more than seeing how so much has changed and much that has not. Looking back over John's life, I recognize how God has dealt with him precisely as He deals with His nation of Israel (and us). We are often rebellious, bring shame to His holy name, and take the hard road. Still, He never gives up on us or abandons us. Instead, He remains God, pursuing His children with unrelenting affection and passion.

Through discipline, blessings, or watching us run off into the wilderness, God refuses to renounce His own. You can rest secure in that!

> *I say then, has God cast away His people? Certainly not!*
> **ROMANS 11:1**

Got It!

How has God enriched your understanding of security through this stone?

_____

_____

_____

_____

It's time to *Dig Deeper!* What is your heart's response to such an unreasonable love that God feels for you? With so many areas of uncertainty and insecurity in the world today, how blessed we are to have a fortified tower to run to. I hope you'll take some time to reflect on this stone and meditate on the scriptures below:

> *"Set your mind on things above, not on things on the earth.*
> *For you died, and your life is hidden with Christ in God."*
> **COLOSSIANS 3:2-3**

> *"I have set the Lord always before me; because*
> *He is at my right hand I shall not be moved."*
> **PSALM 16:8**

"I am the door. If anyone enters by Me, he will be saved, and will go in and out and find pasture... I am the good shepherd. The good shepherd gives His life for the sheep."

JOHN 10:9,11

In the space below, record what new concepts you added to your foundation of security by digging deeper:

Salvation

*Lord, to whom shall we go? You have the words of eternal life.
Also we have come to believe and know that You are the Christ,
the Son of the living God.*

JOHN 6:68-69

Many are the souls who have prayed and accepted Christ. But as I often tell people, it isn't the prayer that saves you, but the attitude of your heart that produces conversion. Please don't confuse salvation with a feeling, though many people have overwhelming emotions of relief, joy, and hope at the moment of transformation. Instead, salvation is rooted and secured in The Word—that is, Jesus Christ.

If you are someone who hasn't given their life over to Jesus, and are not familiar with the words, "I am the way, the truth, and the life. No one comes to the Father except through Me" (John 14:6), then you are lacking the foundational Cornerstone needed for a solid Christian faith. It is on this very Cornerstone that all the other foundational stones rest upon.

Coming to the place where you are willing to trade your personal ambitions—to give away your old life for a new one that is a complete mystery—could be the scariest thing you will ever do. Maybe that's why it's so much easier for a child to accept Jesus. As children, we have little to lose in the way of personal assets or intellectual investments. However, when we grow into adults and begin to accumulate a store of worldly views and opinions, self-serving goals, and physical and emotional desires, we are embedded in belongings we wouldn't dream of giving up.

In the list of material and mental properties we cling to, control is probably the most terrifying thing we are expected to surrender. Who in their right mind would want to renounce their own power under any circumstances, let alone to an invisible being they can't see, hear, or feel? To those who have not been "called" by God, it's an absolutely crazy notion. Still, how can we explain the millions of souls—the poor, the wealthy, the uneducated and scholars, the powerless and the powerful—who have gone on to achieve great things in the company of this covert God?

One explanation can be found in a quote by a favorite Irish-born lay theologian, literary scholar, and author, Clive Staples Lewis.

> *If we discover a desire within us that nothing in this world can satisfy,*
> *also, we should begin to wonder if perhaps we were*
> *created for another world.*
> **C.S. LEWIS**

Is that something that resonates with you? Have you ever felt like an alien in a foreign land where no amount of money, toys, or accomplishments have satisfied an emptiness inside? Are you being called right now?

Do you question whether you are saved or not?

If the Spirit of God dwells within you, you'll know it. Nothing is more important to you than that of the will of God. But if you're not sure, ask Him to take your hand and lead you into a special place with Him.

Just as the Israelites crossed the Jordan on dry ground and set up twelve stones as a memorial for all God had done for them, He also wants to take you from the old to the new, from the mud of your past onto the dry ground He has laid out before you filled with extraordinary possibilities.

> *Examine yourselves as to whether you are in the faith. Test yourselves.*
> *Do you not know yourselves, that Jesus Christ is in you?*
> *—unless indeed you are disqualified.*
> **2 CORINTHIANS 13:5**

The beautiful thing about going through with this frightening act of submission, is that a marvelous happening occurs—the entering and abiding of the Holy Spirit.

If you have ever felt completely alone, if you have found yourself misunderstood or ridiculed, if you have seldom had a sense of family, these will radically change as you enter the presence of the Lord. You are instantly accepted and adopted into a heavenly family as well as an earthly family of fellow believers. You will begin to enjoy the benefits of being a "new creature" in Christ, an heir to the riches of heaven, and will grow in areas you never thought possible.

There is a power that comes with the Holy Spirit that can only be described as supernatural love. As a vital member of the Trinity, the Holy Spirit is the part of God who is here with us on earth. With the Father in heaven and Jesus at His right side, the Spirit of God was sent to be with us every minute of every day until Jesus returns. The Spirit is described as God's "seal" to identify us when Christ comes to claim His own.

The Spirit has God's omniscient foreknowledge of your future, and will guide and protect you. He is your Friend who only has your very best interests in mind. He guarantees your inheritance is secured for the day of redemption. The Spirit is your Father's warm hug when the coldness of this life sets in.

You will never be alone again.

> *For you were bought at a price; therefore, glorify God in your body and in your spirit, which are God's.*
> **1 CORINTHIANS 6:20**

If you have never given your life to Jesus, or perhaps you did long ago and want to renew your vow, I ask that you get on your knees right now and pray this simple prayer:

> *Dear Father in heaven, I admit that I've ignored You, and that I've lived my life on my own terms and I'm asking You now to forgive me for that. Expunge my record of past wrongs. I admit that Jesus was already convicted for my sins, took the blame, and was put to death for them. Only He could do it—live a perfect life worthy of a child of God—and in my acknowledgment of that, He has made me clean. I am no longer a sinner, but a saint in Your sight. I now invite the Holy Spirit to come and live inside me, until the day I see Jesus face to face. Thank You, Father, for this undeserved favor. Draw me ever closer to You. I pray this in Jesus's holy name. Amen.*

How does it feel to be free?

Now go, be with like-minded people. Stay in the Word of God and pray every day. There is no time, place, or occasion when you cannot talk to God. His door is always open. His affection for you, unconditional and never ending. As His child, you are now never without help, without hope, or without Him.

The Lord bless you and keep you;
the Lord make His face shine upon you, and be gracious to you;
the Lord lift up His countenance upon you, and give you peace.

NUMBERS 6:24-26

ORDER INFORMATION

To order individual copies go to
redemption-press.com/bookstore

For discounts on bulk orders
send an email to
bookorders@redemption-press.com.
subject: bulk orders